# *Reviews*

o o o o o o o o o o o o o o o o o o o o o o o o o o o o o o o o o

"*Grace Amid Tragedy* is a beautiful memoir that rises above the spectacular clips and sound bites to connect the reader with the real gravity of Hurricane Katrina. Jim Clark provides a stirring, honest view of his two-week tenure as assistant manager of a Red Cross shelter in Gulfport, Mississippi, just days after the storm. I was left with much more than information about a tragedy. Something peered through the pages to remind me that when everything is stripped bare, we find something we have always looked for—we find hope."

—*Mitch Majeski, Pastor,*
*Summitview Community Church*

o o o o o o o o o o o o o o o o o o o o o o o o o o o o o o o o o

"If you're seeking more purpose and meaning in your life this book is an inspiring guide. Jim Clark describes the humanity-in-action he experienced when he responded to 'the strongest delivered Divine dispatch' in his life. Inexorably drawn to frontline relief work in the aftermath of Hurricane Katrina, Clark witnessed incredible suffering but also powerful acts of compassion. His experiences make us all feel more alive, connected, and open to our own intuitive, wake-up calls."

—*Susan Skog, author.*

# Grace Amid Tragedy

# Grace Amid Tragedy

◆

## A Red Cross Volunteer
## on the Katrina Frontline

*Jim D. Clark*

iUniverse, Inc.
New York Lincoln Shanghai

# Grace Amid Tragedy
## A Red Cross Volunteer on the Katrina Frontline

iUniverse books may be ordered through booksellers or by contacting:

iUniverse
2021 Pine Lake Road, Suite 100
Lincoln, NE 68512
www.iuniverse.com
1-800-Authors (1-800-288-4677)

ISBN-13: 978-0-595-40098-0 (pbk)
ISBN-13: 978-0-595-84482-1 (ebk)
ISBN-10: 0-595-40098-1 (pbk)
ISBN-10: 0-595-84482-0 (ebk)

Printed in the United States of America

This book is dedicated to the many Hurricane Katrina victims who demonstrated not only emotional strength and courage in confronting their losses, but also compassion in helping other victims.

# Contents

# *Acknowledgements*

A journal reflecting the spiritual growth derived through helping others in critical need and establishing close relationships would be quite suspect if it did not include a recognition and expression of gratitude to the very people who fostered that growth. To begin with, I want to convey my admiration and respect to the American Red Cross organization for the invaluable disaster relief services that they provide in this country and world-wide, and for providing me with the medium through which I had this memorable and profound experience. They are a truly remarkable and essential non-profit agency, and they deserve the public's full support. What they accomplish with volunteer labor is astounding.

Although Hurricane Katrina was a devastating tragedy which cannot be completely offset, I do believe with all of my heart and soul that much good is coming from it, and I strongly suspect divine involvement plays a part. I observed monumental displays of compassion and spiritual growth, and I personally experienced it in a way that has fundamentally altered my life. It does not erase all of the loss, pain and suffering, but it sure softens it and makes the best of a horrid situation. For the growth that I experienced, I am forever indebted to the strength, courage, and sharing of the hurricane victims that I met, in particular Julio, Cowboy, Clare, and especially Anna. I pray for their—and all of the hurricane victims'—continued recoveries.

Much of the richness and depth of my experience, both while in Gulfport and afterward in the processing and writing phase, can be attributed to several of the Red Cross volunteers that I met, especially George Estes, Jill Siegel, Carrie Williams, and Dawn Misawic. I can only hope that my life has touched them equally.

During my journey of writing this narrative and getting it published I was touched and strengthened by the support of others. Having had no previous experience with writing professionally, I lacked a reference point to assess the quality of my writing and the foundation to stand confidently. Julio, Dawn, my parent-in-laws Ron and Betsy Barnes, and friends Mitch Majeski and Susan Skog provided all of the encouragement that was required, uncannily at just the right times.

John Pratt, Fran Johnson, Ellen Viens, and Barb Smith graciously volunteered their time and expertise to proofread and copyedit my manuscript. Their general comments and grammatical corrections significantly improved the finished product. I am extremely appreciative of their efforts.

My wife, Lisa Barnes, provided resolute loving support through the many-month duration of being in Gulfport and writing about it, and in fact, has done so throughout my evolving search for meaning over the past 25 years. Dylan and Austin, my two wonderful sons, teach me so much about the many facets of love and spiritual growth that it is a book in itself. Early on in the writing of the manuscript for this book, a computer glitch vaporized a full day's worth of my writing. I was thoroughly despondent about it, and seriously considered abandoning the project. Lisa, Dylan, and Austin all resolutely buoyed me, and cheered loudly when I pulled out of it and announced that I would persevere and re-write the lost portion. A triangle is the strongest structural geometry for support, and Lisa, Dylan and Austin provide the three points of the framework from which I find most of the meaning in my life.

# *Prologue*

o o o o o o o o o o o o o o o o o o o o o o o o o o o o o o o o o o o o

*"I fell through a nightmare, but God caught me."*

—*Julio Morban, Hurricane Katrina victim.*

On September 11<sup>th</sup>, 2006, less than two weeks after Katrina hit, I arrived in Gulfport, Mississippi as an excited and semi-nervous American Red Cross rookie volunteer. With the prevalence of the national media's attention on the massive destruction caused by the flooding damage in New Orleans, I, along with the general public, was not nearly as familiar with Katrina's impact on the Mississippi coast, 40 to 100 miles east of New Orleans. It was this area, however, in communities such as Waveland, Biloxi, and Gulfport, that was ground zero for the hurricane's 145 mile per hour winds and 30-foot storm surge.

Most of what was previously built on that 60-mile coastline, for at least one-quarter mile inland, was thoroughly obliterated. The elementary-school-turned-shelter in which I served as assistant manager is located within that coastal strip, no more than one mile from the ocean.

It has been said that Hurricane Katrina cannot be captured in any single story; that it is actually a compilation of at least 500,000 tragic stories from each of its victims. That belief is inaccurate on two accounts. Although all of those victims' stories undoubtedly did begin as tales of hardship and misfortune, many have more recently been softened with additional chapters describing the extraordinary good will and compassion bestowed upon them by neighbors and absolute strangers from every corner of the country, and even the occasional instance of a life changed for the better. Furthermore, to obtain a truly accurate picture of Hurricane Katrina, one must also consider the stories of literally hundreds of thousands of volunteers who assisted with the relief and rebuilding effort, and how their lives were changed for the better.

Although this memoir is but one more story to add to so many others, it tries to incorporate the breadth of both hurricane victims and volunteers. It is also a view that recognizes Hurricane Katrina as not only the most destructive natural disaster in the history of the United States, but also the catalyst for the largest outpouring of donations, volunteers, and compassion in our country's history.

I did not so much decide to volunteer with Katrina as I felt compelled to volunteer. It was the first sense of a spiritual calling in my 50 years of life, and I simply answered the call. I followed that potent urge, took advantage of all of the subsequent opportunities that seemingly fell in my lap, and ended up being in the right place at the right time to have a substantial impact on people's lives. I feel incredibly blessed to have had the opportunity to make a difference. Making this experience even more influential in my life was the fact that it corresponded with being in the throes of an active search for a greater sense of purpose and meaning. When I submitted to that gripping force to turn onto the hurricane-relief-effort path, it's now evident that it provided many of the answers that I was seeking. It has set a whole new direction for my life; one that began unfolding with the publishing of this book and the associated donation of 50 percent of the proceeds to the hurricane recovery effort.

Perhaps you are also part of the Hurricane Katrina story as one of its victims, a volunteer, or a donor. Or, maybe you are considering volunteering to assist with the reconstruction phase, which will be needed for years to come. We can all learn from this still-unfolding story; perhaps the two most important lessons being the incredible potential that resides within each of us to overcome life's hardships through our beliefs and our actions, along with the immense value of reaching out to support others. It is my hope that through reading this book you find the inspiration to reap more of that potential and value within your own life.

**Notes:**

This book is not sponsored, endorsed or authorized by the American Red Cross. Consistent with American Red Cross confidentiality policy and out of common courtesy, the names for all hurricane victims and Red Cross volunteers are pseudonyms and identifying descriptions have been avoided, other than when I was given specific permission.

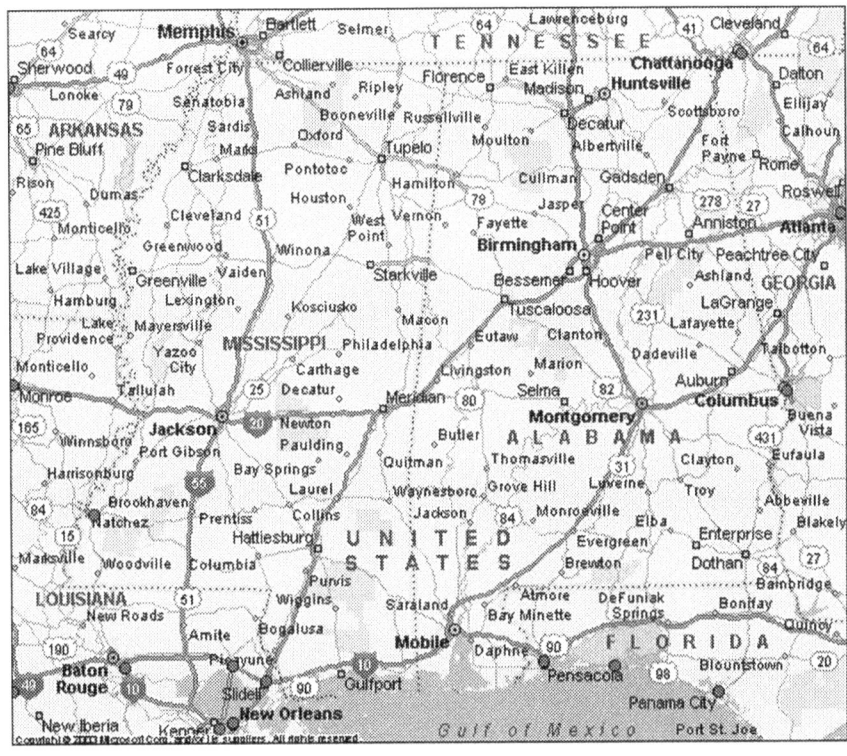

# 1

# *Catastrophe and a Calling*

### *Thursday, August 25, 2005*

*Tropical storm Katrina is upgraded to become Hurricane Katrina, the fourth hurricane of the 2005 season. It makes landfall near Hallandale, Florida as a category 1, coursing south along the Florida coast and then west into the Gulf of Mexico. Because of its relatively low strength, the death total in Florida is limited to 14.*

### *Friday, August 26*

*The National Hurricane Center forecasts that Katrina will strike the town of Buras, east of New Orleans. The prediction later turns out to be off by only 14 miles. In anticipation of a major hurricane, the National Red Cross sends out requests to local chapters around the country to deliver equipment to the staging area of Little Rock, Arkansas. Twelve hundred miles from New Orleans, in Fort Collins, Colorado, where I live, our local Red Cross chapter responds by dispatching its emergency response truck and a driver.*

### Saturday, August 27

*Hurricane Katrina reaches Category 3 intensity, with sustained winds of 115 miles per hour. Concern is rapidly increasing about the potential for this to become a catastrophic storm, in terms of both power and damage.*

### Sunday, August 28

*Slowly moving over the unusually warm waters of the Gulf of Mexico, Hurricane Katrina rapidly grows in strength. At 12:40 a.m., it is a Category 4 storm, with sustained winds of 135 miles per hour. By 7:00 a.m., it has reached Category 5, with sustained winds of 175 mph and gusts to 216 mph. The National Weather Service issues a bulletin predicting devastating damage.*

Over the previous several days, I had become increasingly riveted by the news of the approaching hurricane. For as long as I can remember, I have been excessively attracted to the extremes of nature and their violent splendor. It feels like an innate, genetic-coded type of urge, which seems reasonable, given that for all but a few of our thousands of generations of human existence, our daily survival has hinged on our adeptness at recognizing and adapting to nature's forces. For most of us, our material wealth and technology now enable us to stay safe and comfortable, relegating nature to a museum display outside our windows. However, a mere handful of generations of "controlling" nature has not eliminated this hard-wired fear, respect, and awe. When on occasion nature does re-assert its dominance, we are shaken out of our predictable and controlled world, and we are reminded of what it means to be humbled and awed, and in the presence of a God-scale event.

Of course, the opportunity to experience these events is a function of time and place. Growing up in the Kansas City area, I experienced thunderstorms, floods, tornadoes, and ice storms. While living in Oregon in 1980 and 1981, I saw coast-battering waves, heavy snows in the Cascades, and the eruption of Mount St. Helens. At home in Fort Collins for the past 24 years, I've lived through limb-breaking snowstorms, hail up to baseball-size, and the Spring Creek flood of 1997.

I would be quick to add that my enthrallment with the excesses of nature is conflicted with a strong empathy when those forces directly affect human lives through loss of property or worse. During a flash flood on the night of July 29, 1997, my residential street became the conduit for a raging torrent with two-foot standing waves that carried several cars hundreds of yards. After my wife and I carried our two-and five-year-old boys through the water to higher ground, the next hour became a surreal experience of the sights and sounds of the two-car garage across the street getting torn from its slab foundation and demolished, along with a freight train derailing and a liquor store exploding from a natural gas leak, only a quarter mile away. At one point I noticed a neighbor woman flashing her porch light across the street, yelling to me in a panic. The flooding water was up to her porch with her car pushed from her driveway downstream to the front yard. "Just stay inside! Don't try to leave the house," I screamed back.

It was pointless, as the deafening noise of the rushing water was overwhelming. Trying to get closer so that she could hear, I took a few tentative steps farther out into the several-foot-deep current, maybe 15 feet from the front of our home. Immediately swept from my feet, I was underwater and being swept away before my reactions could prevent it. While it was only a matter of seconds before I was able to grab the trunk of a small tree and regain my footing, it was a panic-filled experience nonetheless.

The water quickly receded, and I spent most of the remainder of the night assisting neighbors and starting to deal with the debris and damage to our garage, crawl space, and yard. After a few hours of sleep, I awoke early to the distinctive sound of helicopters, some being used for searching and some by the media. A short while later, search and rescue personnel on horseback came down our street, each holding a long white pole used for body searches in water and debris piles.

As it turned out, five lives were sadly lost, along with many millions of dollars in property damage along the creek corridor and on the Colorado State University campus. While I don't think that I was previously insensitive to the human trauma caused by natural disasters, having that personal experience most certainly made me acutely aware of the intensity of emotion involved.

## Monday, August 29

*At 6:10 a.m., Hurricane Katrina makes its landfall near Buras, Louisiana, with sustained winds of 145 mph, a strong Category 4 storm. Its lowest minimum pressure at landfall is 27.11 inches, making it the third strongest hurricane on record to make landfall in the United States. This hurricane is not only extremely powerful, it is also enormous in size. In the northeast quadrant of the hurricane—the most damaging side—a 10- to 30-foot storm surge comes ashore on over 200 continuous miles of coastline, along the shores of southeast Louisiana, Mississippi, Alabama, and the Florida panhandle. The 30-foot storm surge recorded at Biloxi, Mississippi is the highest ever observed in America. Record storm surges that had not occurred in at least the previous 150 years inundated the entire Mississippi coastline, destroying many thousands of buildings.*

I found myself obsessed with monitoring news of the hurricane and its aftermath. National Public Radio broadcasts, television networks, and various web sites covering the topic only served to fan the flames of my fascination. It felt as if some mysterious, unsettled force was building within me, but I was having trouble identifying it.

### Tuesday, August 30

*An estimated one and one-half million people are now evacuated from their homes in Louisiana, Mississippi, and Alabama. Yesterday most of New Orleanians felt that they had dodged a bullet by not suffering more significant damage from Katrina's direct impact of wind and storm surge. Overnight, however, several significant levees protecting New Orleans were breached, including one holding back Lake Pontchartrain. It is reported that 80 percent of New Orleans is now under water.*

*News video footage shows some of the worst devastation, not only to New Orleans but to the Mississippi coast in the area of Biloxi and Gulfport. From the reporting, there is a distinction between the damage in the two regions. New Orleans' catastrophic damage was rendered primarily by the immense flooding caused by the breached levees and the fact that it is a densely populated area, rather than the storm surge itself or wind. Greater numbers of deaths are being reported and anticipated for this area. Additional public interest results from New Orleans' status as a unique cultural icon. In contrast, damage to the Mississippi coast was caused primarily by the massive storm surge and hurricane-force winds, resulting in more physical devastation. Video and photographs of the Mississippi coast dramatically show that the many large casinos previously floating just offshore were washed hundreds of yards inland and decimated. Most of the bridges spanning the small bays in the region were extensively damaged. U.S. 90, the commercial east/west beach boulevard that ran right along the boardwalk in Biloxi and Gulfport now looked like infrequent sections of asphalt and piles of debris and sand, rather than a road.*

With the news in New Orleans seemingly going from bad to worse by the hour, I recalled that I read an article in the October, 2004 issue of *National Geographic* entitled, "Gone with the Water," about the catastrophic consequences of a major hurricane hitting New Orleans. I did some web-surfing and located a more scholarly article in the *Natural Hazards Observer*, entitled "What if Hurricane Ivan had not missed New Orleans?" Both articles eerily predicted exactly what was happening in this hurricane.

Mesmerized by the horrid images, I began to think about my options for helping to alleviate the pain and suffering.

## Wednesday, August 31

*The grim enormity of the devastation inflicted by Hurricane Katrina became apparent today in battered, reeling New Orleans and the Mississippi Coast. President Bush flew over the disaster area in Air Force One, and he later spoke on live television. "We are dealing with one of the worst natural disasters in our nation's history," said Bush, who pledged to send personnel, supplies, and money to aid the relief effort. Federal officials declared a public health emergency for the entire Gulf Coast, and rushed food, medicine, and water to the victims, in one of the largest relief efforts in US history. In a plan organized by the Pentagon, four Navy ships were dispatched to the Gulf Coast, along with the hospital ship USNS Comfort, search helicopters, and elite SEAL water-rescue teams. To bolster that effort, the US military will send an additional 10,000 National Guard troops to Louisiana and Mississippi, bringing to 28,000 the total number of active-duty Army and National Guard troops deployed in the four-state coast from Louisiana to Florida. American Red Cross workers from across the country converged on the region in what the agency called its largest domestic relief operation ever.*

*In New Orleans, officials estimated that 80,000 people remained in the city, out of a total population of 480,000. Mayor Ray Nagin ordered the entire city evacuated. "We have to," the mayor said. "The city will not be functional for two or three months." As part of the evacuation, officials planned a two-day convoy of 475 buses to carry people who have been sheltered in the Superdome to Houston, 350 miles away. Tempers had begun to flare in the complex, where Katrina punched holes in the roof, and many toilets stopped working. As National Guard and police patrolled flooded streets, looters ransacked stores throughout the city, carrying away enormous quantities of food, clothing, appliances, and guns. Last night, the mayor ordered 1,500 police to leave their search-and-rescue missions to stop the looting. Meanwhile, the water appears to have stopped rising in the city, and the Army Corps of Engineers struggled to repair damaged levees. It is estimated that it will take at least 30 days to pump the water back into the lake. "The magnitude of our work is unfathomable," Louisiana Governor Kathleen Blanco said. "We need a higher power now."*

Hearing stories and seeing news footage of dead bodies being left alongside roads for days made me literally feel ill. It was a surreal image that I knew happens in other parts of the world but not in the United States. I felt guilty in recognizing that I was more deeply moved by it occurring in my country than I was when it occurred elsewhere.

I was so saddened, numbed, and obsessed with this tragedy that I began to feel an unprecedented urge to take action. "I can't *not* go," I thought to myself. Part of the attraction was admittedly my affinity to experience and see the results of nature's extremes. However, by far the strongest component of this compelling force was to get myself in a position to make a tangible and direct difference. Despite my understanding that financial donations are essential and very worthy support, I felt that a contribution alone would do absolutely nothing to fulfill this calling.

My first thought was to consider the American Red Cross because of its extensive experience in disaster relief. I called the Fort Collins office of our regional Red Cross chapter to obtain the basic information on the process for becoming a volunteer deployed to the disaster area. "Our primary need right now is with operating the hundreds of shelters that we've set up around the country," the volunteer receptionist informed me. He continued with his explanation. "We're fast-tracking our training, and you'll need to take three training sessions of two to three hours each on the subjects of Orientation, Mass Care Overview and Shelter Operations. That's followed with an individual deployment interview. You could complete all of this within five days, if you're willing and able." Through the remainder of our conversation, I learned that they required a commitment to be deployed for at least two weeks, and certain minimum qualifications had to be met for health and suitability. This particular assignment was described as an "extreme hardship" deployment, given that it would likely involve unsanitary conditions with no electricity, no potable water, hot and humid weather, exposure to extreme emotional duress, and limited ability to reach friends and family by phone. The earliest deployment could start as soon as the following week. Although all of the time would be unpaid, no expenses would be incurred by volunteers, as Red Cross pays for the travel expenses, and a debit card would be issued to cover relevant and appropriate expenses.

My wife Lisa and I talked about our feelings of despair over the evolving disaster. She was also struggling with how best to help. I shared with her my strong desire to go through the Red Cross training, and if it seemed like a good fit, to make a two-week commitment to help operate a shelter in some unknown, out-of-state location. I knew that my leaving for two weeks would have a large impact on her, as she would have to do double-duty for tasks related to parenting our two boys, ages 10 and 13, along with the other household chores that I usually cover. She gave me her unconditional support, saying that she could indirectly help the relief effort by creating the opportunity for me to do so.

We then talked with our boys about it. Lisa and I have raised them with the value of service to others and the importance of volunteer work. For example, each of them volunteers once per month with Lisa or me to prepare and serve dinner at the local homeless shelter. They also often voluntarily help out neighbors. Still, this was taking it one large step further. Their initial reaction was fear, especially when imagining that I would be wading through the toxic waters of New Orleans searching for bodies, with renegade looters and anarchy all about. I assured them that my assignment would be far safer, and that I would use my good judgment to avoid excessive risks. That helped, and their thoughts turned to the exciting and adventurous aspects of it, which they could vicariously experience. I could also see a dose of pride in the tone of their voices and expressions, and that made me feel good. I had never been separated from either of them for more than six days, so we all knew that it would be challenging in that respect.

## Thursday, September 1

*Bodies continue to be pulled from the rubble in Gulfport and Biloxi, along the Mississippi coast. Hundreds of people are still being rescued from New Orleans. The shelter in Houston's Astrodome is ruled to be full and cannot accept any more evacuees from the New Orleans Superdome.*

*With the distressing news about the longer-term need for housing hundreds of thousands of hurricane evacuees, thousands of people around the country are offering up their homes for free lodging. A number of websites are launched to match those offering housing to those in need of it. Some government officials express safety concerns about strangers being placed in private homes, but it does not temper grass-roots enthusiasm. One listing in Fort Collins reads: "Family will help you get here. One hour north of Denver. Free room and board for motivated student or single mom with one school-age child while you get on your feet. Nice home and community. We have dogs and cats. May you be surrounded by love and light during this difficult time."*

The next step in my consideration of volunteering with the Red Cross involved making sure that it would work out with my employment. My intent was to take the two weeks as vacation time, as I had an adequate amount cumulated. I considered my work responsibilities and schedule and knew that my presence was not urgently needed until late September. When I discussed the idea with my boss and my three staff members, all were very supportive. It seemed that a door was opening for me. I was excited and somewhat anxious to walk through it.

### Friday, September 2

*People in some areas of the Mississippi and Louisiana coasts are still waiting for rescue, food, and/or water. The media reports a great deal of confusion, slow delivery of service, and woefully inadequate communication. The areas hardest hit by the hurricane are largely populated with low-income people, with a high percentage being black, initiating a fervent national discussion and debate about related issues of race and inequity. Criticism mounts, with the strongly-expressed opinion that the disaster is being greatly exacerbated by wretched poverty that our society has decided to accept or chosen to ignore. A poll conducted by the Pew Center for the People and the Press found that 26 percent of whites agreed that the government response would have been faster if most of the victims had been white, whereas 66 percent of blacks agreed with that statement.*

*In Fort Collins, Pat Stryker, president of the Bohemian Foundation, announces a promise to match every dollar donated for the hurricane relief to either the Community Foundation of Northern Colorado or United Way of Larimer County through September 17th. "The country came to our aid in 1997 after the Spring Creek flood," she said. "Now, we're giving back to the country."*

My first two hours of Red Cross training took place at the Fort Collins branch office of the Red Cross's Centennial chapter. The office is located in a residential neighborhood with 30 to 40-year-old homes, and shows every indication of being a modest quality home that was donated to the Red Cross years ago, and remodeled for office use. It is a split-level, and the training room is located on the upper level.

I was part of the first wave of about 15 volunteers being trained. The training room is large enough to seat perhaps 50 people with chairs and no tables, but for this training they have set it up with eight or nine standard two-foot by eight-foot folding tables in a U-shaped configuration. We sat around the perimeter looking over the handout material and visiting while waiting for the class to begin. Only two of my fellow volunteers appeared close to my age; the others were either in their 20's or of retirement age. The gender mix was approximately two-thirds male and one-third female. With the beginning of the training we each briefly introduced ourselves, with everyone expressing in various ways how we were saddened by the news and wanted to help alleviate the pain and suffering in a hands-on manner. At least half were employed or trained in an emergency responder or medical field.

As with most Red Cross operations the training was handled by a volunteer. In this case it was Bonnie, a soft-spoken woman that appeared to be in her early 60's. She began by mentioning that it was the first time that she had led a training session, and she did seem a little nervous with the role. However, the audience was understanding and supportive towards her, and she ended up doing a fine job. Through the orientation video and literature, I learned that the International Red Cross movement began in the 1860's through the actions of one man, Henri Dunant, a Swiss businessman. While traveling in northern Italy he had witnessed the Battle of Solferino between the French and the Austrians, in which 40,000 troops were killed or wounded and left on the battlefield without help. The sight horrified him and he mobilized the local citizens to bury the dead and help the wounded. On his return to Geneva he wrote about the experience, which resulted in the birth of the International Red Cross.

Clara Barton, a former school teacher, is credited with founding the American Red Cross in 1881 after personally caring for wounded soldiers in the Civil War and the Franco-Prussian War in Europe. A Congressional mandate is now in place designating the Red Cross to work with federal agencies in aiding victims of natural disasters. The Red Cross is guided by seven fundamental principles, including humanity, impartiality, neutrality, independence, voluntary service, unity, and universality. The five primary service areas in the Red Cross are Armed Forces Emergency Services, Biomedical Services (including blood collecting and distribution for 50 percent of the public), Health and Safety Services (including first aid, CPR and babysitting training), International Services, and Disaster Services. It is in this latter area that we were being trained.

Most people—including myself—probably first associate American Red Cross relief work with major disasters, such as floods, tornadoes, and hurricanes. That certainly occurs, but the majority of local Red Cross chapters are involved in smaller-scale, local relief needs, such as single-family or apartment fires. When there is a larger, regional or national-scale disaster, there is an established protocol for the impacted local chapters to secure assistance and involvement from the national office.

Toward the end of the first meeting, several of us asked questions. Paramount on my mind was the question of when we would know our ultimate destination. "At your departure time, you will only know your initial staging area, probably

Houston, Texas, Baton Rouge, Louisiana, or Montgomery, Alabama. After arriving there, you will then be assigned either to that regional headquarters or more likely to another location within that region," was the response from our trainer. Only a small degree of flexibility would exist to either accept or deny and wait for another possible assignment. At the end of the meeting, we went over the intended schedule for the next week's training sessions. At this time I planned to go to the second training session on Monday (Labor Day), the last training session on Tuesday, have my deployment interview on Wednesday, and be ready to fly out on Friday, September 9.

### Saturday, September 3

*In the hurricane's aftermath, federal disaster declarations now blanket 90,000 square miles of the United States, an area larger than the state of Minnesota. Homeland Security Secretary Michael Chertoff described this as "the worst natural catastrophe in our country's history."*

*With nearly 90 percent of the Gulf states' oil production capacity out of service, the national average for gas hits $3.07, breaking the historical record after adjusting for inflation.*

In retrospect this weekend served as a pivotal transition point in my spiritual life. During the previous six months I had come to realize that I needed to re-establish my sense of purpose and life meaning, and that my typical methods for doing so were not working. My decision had been made to follow my calling, with the training begun. The training would continue on Monday, and I would likely be on my way by the end of the next week. I would later realize that my two-week Red Cross experience and its aftermath transformed my spiritual life, and provide many of the answers that I was seeking. Perhaps with a sense of being at a nexus point, I spent a good portion of my available time during this weekend reflecting on where I had been, and where I wanted to be.

The most obvious and potent catalyst for my recent spiritual malaise was my 50th birthday last spring. Prior to this event, my age had never really been an issue for me. "Just a number," as the saying goes. Being blessed with good health, maintaining my fitness, looking young for my years, and having a youthful attitude towards life had allowed me to keep thoughts of my mortality at bay. Still, there has been a gradual progression of realizing the inevitable. In my twenties, I lived life as if I were immortal. Sure, I knew that I would eventually die, but it was so far out there that it was a safely abstract concept. My youthful armor lost its luster and a few chinks appeared in it during my thirties and forties, and I would characterize my perspective as becoming "semi-mortal" during those years. Now, after passing the fifty-year mark, and more importantly experiencing the thoughts and feelings stimulated by that fact, I fully grasp that I am undeniably and unequivocally mortal. It is more than a cognitive awareness; it is a core emotional and spiritual understanding. Although I may yet live another 30 or 40 years, I also began to fully comprehend that I might not live to see the next sunrise. This heightened state of consciousness may more typically be spurred by a physical brush with death, but why can't it also be triggered by spiritual reflection and the influences of a Higher Power?

That revision of perspective immediately caused me to feel a sense of instability, like a wheel out of balance suddenly creating a noisy and rough ride. Initially, a feeling of great urgency overtook me. It felt absolutely imperative for me to complete my purpose, to fully live every moment, and to no longer hold back. It became essential that I live with boldness and courage, and that I make the most substantial difference of which I am capable. Anything less would feel completely unacceptable.

Following closely on the heels of the sense of urgency was an equally visceral anxiety. In order to fulfill my purpose and to sing my song, I would obviously need to know what my purpose was, and to have the melody and lyrics for my song, and I knew I didn't. To add another layer to the challenge, I had been struggling for a long time with the very *process* for ascertaining my purpose. If determining one's purpose was only a straightforward function of intense desire, hard work, and perseverance, I would have it nailed. But I had been down that road, giving it my all, yet the sense of an unfulfilled calling and a withering of my soul remained. An alarm was sounding, loud and clear, that I could and should be making a more meaningful difference in the world. The alarm had my attention; I was fully awake and motivated to make the necessary changes. But what changes? I needed direction. The darkness of depression—an occasional, un-welcomed force—made its presence known, adversely affecting my relationships and other aspects of my life. I read self-help and spiritually-oriented books, I reflected, I prayed; all seemingly to no avail.

## Sunday, September 4

*It is estimated that the hurricane left five million people without power. The projected cost of the damage and recovery is now at $200 to $300 billion, dwarfing the $70 bil-*

*lion cost (adjusted for inflation) of Hurricane Andrew as the country's previously most expensive natural disaster.*

*Along with many other colleges and universities across the country, Colorado State University in Fort Collins has offered late enrollment and financial aid to displaced students from the Gulf Coast. Numerous local citizens have offered free housing to such students.*

On occasion I have envied people that have no urge or need to search for meaning in their lives, whether due to having a firm and satisfied grip on their definition of it, or even due to it being altogether off their radar screen. However, for me and I suspect many others it is really a life-long process, with no precise beginning and end points. "Meaning" becomes a moving target, as catalyzed by various life events and personal growth.

Still, there are active, less active and dormant phases of a lifelong search, with general themes associated with each active phase. My soul awakened on the heels of adolescence, between the ages of 18 and 20. Through my reading and spiritual work, I gradually gained a stronger sense of connection to my soul, rather than to my personality and ego. I viewed my soul as being the hub of my being, and my personality as more of a mask and bound up with inaccurate judgments and perceptions. An often-used quotation in spiritual practices is, "We are spiritual beings having a human experience, rather than human beings trying to have a spiritual experience," and I felt much aligned with that belief. It was the first time that I experienced true spiritual bliss and knew with all of my being that there was an entirely different level of consciousness possible, elevated from all that I had previously experienced. It was a very tangible sense of connecting with Oneness. In my reading during that time, I came upon the Greek word, *Metanoia*, used in the Christian bible and elsewhere. While it literally translates to "a change of mind," in spiritual contexts it is used in a broader manner to mean a change of mind, heart, and character as part of a spiritual transformation whereby God takes center place in our consciousness and awareness. With that being a suitable description for what I had experienced, I came to think of that time period as the Metanoia of my life.

My second active phase of my search for meaning began at the age of 26 in 1981, and was prompted by an intense longing to make a difference in my vocational life. In hindsight, it was a struggle with making my spiritual values "real" and applying them to the physical world. With my analytical and detail-oriented personality, I spent untold hundreds of hours over a five-year period attempting to determine my purpose, through reading nearly every *What Color is Your Para-*

*chute?*[1] type of book available, writing my autobiography, taking numerous tests to assess my aptitudes, interests and values, and much reflecting. I was employed during this entire time, but I did not find it very fulfilling. As a result of all of this, I had a firm idea of who I was, but there still was no enlightened realization of a calling. During this time, I suffered from moderate depression, in large part due to the lack of determining my soul's purpose and in fulfilling it.

Then, in 1986, I visited the Cheyenne Botanic Gardens in Cheyenne, Wyoming, and that seemed to synthesize everything that I had been considering. The Cheyenne Botanic Gardens is a relatively small facility, but it is very unique and extremely impactful in that community. Within their environmentally-friendly greenhouse and on their grounds, they utilize dozens of seniors, people with disabilities, and at-risk youth as volunteers. These volunteers grow many tons of vegetables, with some given to the volunteers and the rest donated to the local food bank. That is complimented with the growing of thousands of annual flower starts that are planted in the city's medians and parks.

This type of facility and associated programming seemed to perfectly match my interest in horticulture, environmental ethic, and desire to make a difference in the community. I became excited with the idea of establishing a similar facility in Fort Collins and immediately set myself to the task of doing so. Eighteen years later, in 2004, we had our Grand Opening at the Gardens on Spring Creek, where I am the director. Through literally thousands of volunteer hours by me and many other supporters, and a successful city vote in 1997 that established the funding, we now have a beautiful building with offices, a greenhouse and a classroom, and an 18-acre site. We have a few acres of environmentally-oriented landscaping and gardens, and we will be adding more as we raise the necessary funds.

It would be reasonable for a person to question why I am feeling a lack of meaning in my life, when I am so fortunate as to not only be in my dream job, but one that I created. I ask myself that same question. Much of my work is enjoyable and there is great satisfaction in knowing that my staff and I bring pleasure, education and fulfilling experiences to our hundreds—and eventually thousands—of visitors and volunteers. Furthermore, I am extremely fortunate to have a wonderful and loving family and caring friends. It is my strong belief that being the best possible husband, father, and friend is where I can have the most positive impact in my life, and I derive considerable meaning from that.

In a way, it does seem a selfish luxury to be in a position to want even more meaning out of my life. The paradox, however, is that I genuinely feel that my desire for more self-fulfillment would be better described as Self-fulfillment, with a capital "S" used to distinguish the more divine aspect of our being, which is fulfilled through serving others and serving God. A part of my being is not being utilized or expressed, and it feels that I am not whole, that a significant something is missing. It is not the type of void that can be fulfilled with more worldly pleasure or ego satisfaction. It is much deeper, at the soul level. While one aspect is that I need to more fully express certain interests and aptitudes, leaving it at that is far too secular. The more accurate sacred perspective is that I need to manifest who I am in order to fulfill a higher purpose. A fitting quote from the Gnostic Gospels, attributed to Jesus, goes, "If you bring forth what is within you, what you bring forth will save you. If you do not bring forth what is within you, what you do not bring forth will destroy you." I feel that to be true, in a very literal sense.

While some people are satisfied with garnering a sense of meaning in their life by shoe-horning it in between work and all of their other routine responsibilities, that is unequivocally not acceptable to me. It is too important—both to the individual and to the condition of our world—to relegate it to such a low priority. Living with a sense of purpose and meaning has to be integrated into one's entire life. My sense of urgency is not only a reflection of my age, it is also an indicator of the critical importance of discerning this purpose and meaning.

These thoughts of mine do not in any way confer a judgment about the value of particular jobs. To the contrary, I firmly believe that any work, as long as it meets common-sense ethical criteria, is potentially soul-fulfilling and can be performed in a manner that truly serves others and God. Even work that is conventionally considered to be menial and lower-status can be accomplished in a way that brings joy and love into the world, if it is done with the right spirit and attitude. A currently popular book, entitled *The Fred Factor: How passion in your work and life can turn the ordinary into the extraordinary²*, is about lessons learned from a postal carrier in Denver who goes far beyond his minimum work duties to emphatically make a difference in hundreds of people's lives. That being acknowledged, I also think that each of us has a calling for a particular type of work, and the better the fit, the easier it is to project a loving spirit and positive attitude to the world.

In this current third active phase of my search for a calling and meaning, I know that I need to take a radically different approach. My previous method took more than two decades to determine and manifest my purpose of establishing the Gardens on Spring Creek, and that timeframe clearly isn't available now. Also, despite my feeling that that was the closest fit for my interests and values, there were never the telltale signs of it being "meant to be." There was no serendipity, no doors opening and seemingly no answers to prayers. It was 22 years of hard, determined and strategic work, overcoming more than a dozen critical challenges when our chances seemed slim. Although I was passionate about fulfilling the dream and what it would bring to the community, the effort was much more cognitive, as opposed to spiritual, intuitive and going with the flow. For this journey, I will be taking the latter tack. That doesn't mean I'm at risk for leaving everything behind and moving to New Zealand to grow kiwis. My rational abilities are still engaged. It only means that I will be making a very determined effort to listen to my inner voice—to God—and that Voice is telling me I need to go help with the hurricane relief.

On one hand, I had not the slightest idea how this two-week commitment could relate to resolving my big picture issue of rediscovering a sense of purpose and meaning in my life. It seemed to be nothing but a diversion or tangent. On the other hand, however, I had an emerging sense that the upcoming experience would not be a mere side path that joined back up to my current life course, but rather a whole new direction for the balance of my years. Furthermore and most significantly, I wasn't about to disobey what felt like the strongest delivered divine dispatch in my life.

## Monday, September 5

*New Orleans Mayor Ray Nagin publicly expresses fear that that the eventual hurricane death toll in his city will be 10,000.*

*News coverage of Katrina's aftermath has become a news item in and of itself. Debate and criticism mounts regarding the appropriateness of graphic images, self-congratulatory reporting by certain television networks, and political bias.*

*Poudre Valley Hospital in Fort Collins is prepared to receive some of the 1,000 hurricane evacuees brought to Denver over the weekend.*

I arrived at the local Red Cross office a little before 2:00 p.m., the supposed start time for the second training session. The room was already filled with about 50 people, obviously in the middle of a training video. Unbeknownst to me, the training schedule had been changed, with all three training sessions condensed even further into one four-to five-hour period. This group had started at 10:00 a.m. and was nearing the end. During that time they had received the training that the other 14 people and I had completed on Friday, in addition to going onward with the remainder. Along with several additional people who had just arrived, also intending to begin the second of three training sessions, we merged ourselves with the group that was in the midst of their training. After the main group of 50 completed their training, those of us who arrived at two o'clock sat through the portion of the video that we had missed.

The training videos informed us on the basics of operating a Red Cross shelter. They were of professional quality, fairly well-acted, and acceptably current. My only suggested improvement would be that the next time the videos (or DVD's) are remade, the producers aim a level or two higher for the assumed educational level of their audience. The current versions seemed too basic and slow, especially given that the handouts covered the exact same material. If the same training that I received had been stretched out over its typical length of time, rather than fast-tracked, I would expect to see some heads nodding off.

Reflective of the unprecedented scope of this national disaster, it was readily apparent that the local chapter was not prepared for training this many people in such a short time. They were doing the best that they could, with well-intentioned and committed staff and volunteers, but the disorganization and lack of preparation was noticeable. Eight forms needed to be completed, and they did not have enough copies. The photocopying process could not keep up. On four or five occasions the volunteer trainers brought in various portions of the forms, and laboriously distributed them to the people who needed them. The process of informing the trainees about how to complete the forms, and the order of assembling them, was chaotic and arduous. Part of my nature and life experience relates to problem-solving and organizing, so my mind gravitated to ideas for making this process smoother and more efficient. Still, I appreciated the fact that these people were working hard and that this situation was very unique. Jason, the Response Director of the local chapter, was impressively balancing a great number of tasks, undoubtedly putting in many extra hours. I saw other volunteers, obviously new at their jobs of answering phones and doing other duties, all with positive attitudes and smiles on their faces.

During one of the brief break periods I had my first tangible, direct sense of the magnitude of this catastrophe. There I was, 1,200 miles away from the area physically damaged by Katrina, but from the hyper-activity and sense of urgency within the building an unknowing observer would have thought the emergency was in the immediate area. Sixty people were being trained on this day, one week after the disaster, and we were just the first of many groups. This same scene was undoubtedly being replicated in hundreds of other cities across the U.S.

In my brief training, I learned that there is a unique lexicon to the Red Cross and a propensity for acronyms and abbreviations. For example, an "ERV" is an emergency response vehicle, the familiar Red Cross box truck that delivers meals and supplies. As a volunteer, I was identified with a DSHR number, an abbreviation for Disaster Services Human Resource. My particular volunteer position would be COS/SH/SA, for Community Services / Shelter Services / Shelter Assistant.

One of our handouts was a list of the items that we were required to bring with us, most notable of which was three days' worth of food and water. This request seemed a bit odd, in that I assumed that a Red Cross shelter, two weeks after a disaster, would have bottled water and food. I concluded that it must be a conservative recommendation and more oriented to covering for the time that might occur before arriving at the shelter. Nevertheless, the recommendation excited me, with its implication that volunteers were being sent to the front line, rather than to a shelter in Houston or some other location more remote from the hurricane-damaged area. Although I had resolved that I would fulfill the commitment regardless of the assigned location, I was eagerly hoping that I would be deployed to the New Orleans area or the Mississippi coast so that I could more directly experience the effects of the disaster and hopefully provide more substantial assistance. Even though I certainly did not consider myself to be experienced and hardened enough to be qualified for the most extreme aspects of the recovery effort, such as search and rescue, I did think that my experience and constitution qualified me for the most extreme situations that a Red Cross shelter would require.

Packing three days' worth of food and water did cause me a mild amount of concern, however, given that, even at the age of 50 and having a thin build, I still have the appetite and metabolism of a ravenous teenager. I am pretty certain that if I wanted to, I could put an all-you-can-eat buffet restaurant out of business with two or three sittings, four max. It would require a single large suitcase just to meet the volume requirements of three days' worth of food and water, not to mention the challenge of carrying that much weight.

In recognition that I was now trained to assist with the operation of a shelter, I was presented with my three Red Cross cards. The last remaining step with the local chapter was the individual deployment interview. In order to schedule that interview, I was told to call after 9:00 a.m. the next morning.

## Tuesday, September 6

*The American Red Cross is now raising money at the fastest pace in its history. Out of all of the money being donated to American charities for Katrina relief, a remarkable 72 percent is going to the Red Cross.*

*"Refugee" becomes a contentious word in referring to Americans who fled from Hurricane Katrina. Some think that "displaced persons" or "evacuee" is more respectful to these Americans because it does not have the same desperate connotations of people fleeing natural disasters or war in Asia and Africa. Others believe that those alternative words are nothing more than euphemisms that sugar-coat the reality of impoverished conditions in the United States.*

Shortly after 9:00 a.m. I called the local chapter. It took several tries to connect, given the volume of calls from potential donors, volunteers, the media, and others. When I finally got through, I was told that they wanted to do the interviews with groups of four and that I should show up at 1:00 p.m. When I arrived, it appeared that the plan for interviews had changed again. Fortunately I was rescued by Connie, one of the local chapter's board members. "Since you're already here, let's just go ahead and get it done," she said. Connie was energetic, very pleasant, and had a wonderful can-do spirit. She assisted me in completing one more form and entered the relevant information on the computer. "The most recent deployments have been to the Montgomery, Alabama headquarters, so there's a good chance they'll ask you to go there," Connie explained. "Someone from this office will call you within 24 hours, after we receive the emailed response from the national headquarters." My excitement escalated as the reality of this adventure and opportunity to help set in.

One of the handouts recommended that we have viable tetanus and hepatitis A shots. My memory was vague on when I had received my last tetanus shot, so I had to call my doctor. Informed that it had been seven years ago, it was within the recommended maximum of ten years. I learned that the hepatitis A is actually a series of two shots given over several weeks, so that obviously could not be accomplished before leaving.

### Wednesday, September 7

*The public's criticism of susceptible infrastructure, inadequate evacuation plans, and slow and inefficient recovery and relief efforts reaches a fever pitch. Charges of ineptitude, corruption, and disregard are leveled at many local, state, and national governmental agencies. Much public wrath has been focused on the Federal Emergency Management Agency and its chief, Michael Brown. Finger-pointing and accusations between all of these agencies are widespread; admitting responsibility and cooperation seem rare. Public confidence in our country's ability to respond to a large-scale terrorist attack reaches its lowest point since the 9/11 tragedy.*

During the late morning, while at work, I got the much-anticipated phone call from the local chapter. I was told that they would like me to go to Montgomery, and I was given a long-distance phone number to call that had a recording with instructions about how to proceed. This recording was continuously updated and included information about the airport that I would fly into, the address of the Red Cross headquarters in Montgomery, the motel that I would go to, ground transportation once I got to Montgomery, additional phone numbers if any problems cropped up, and the strong recommendation to check back at the same recording after I arrived at the airport to see if anything had changed. I was impressed with all of the logistics that must have been involved in keeping this recording—which was likely only one of many—accurate and updated. The local chapter had also instructed me to book my flight through World Travel BTI, which was contracted to handle all of the travel arrangements for Red Cross volunteers nationwide.

I was extremely happy to hear that I would be going to Montgomery, the headquarters for all of the Mississippi and Alabama relief efforts. (Baton Rouge was the headquarters for the Louisiana relief effort, and there was also a headquarters in Houston.) Not only was I one step closer to being able to get deployed to the coast (although that was by no means certain), I would also be going to one of only four of the 48 contiguous states that I had never visited. I arranged my flights, leaving on Friday, September 9th and returning two weeks later on September 23rd.

I began packing my supplies, a relatively easy task compared to packing for family adventures, given that this trip was only for me and the clothing would be very limited. I called the Montgomery headquarters to ask about the need for bringing water. They said that the water service in Montgomery was not disrupted, so I could supply myself with water when I got there and not have to lug it on my flight. I still needed the space for a couple of empty two-liter water bottles, but they were certainly lighter. Just to be safe, I also packed the water filter that I used for backpacking. For food, I decided to focus primarily on my particular food preferences, which could either be used for subsistence if I were in a situation without food, or as a substitute for undesirable food, if our shelter only had something I would find detestable like Velveeta cheese or Spam. With my predilection towards a more nutritious diet, I brought along about five pounds of homemade granola—my standard breakfast—along with powdered milk, peanut butter, whole wheat tortillas, energy bars, honey, V-8 juice, dried fruit, and nuts.

### *Thursday, September 8*

*Now 12 days after Katrina made landfall, the messages on websites and electronic bulletin boards from those searching for lost loved ones are becoming increasingly frantic. More than 117,000 people have registered online with the Family Links registry operated by the American Red Cross, and an additional 45,000 have called the organization's toll-free hotline.*

*Consumer watchdogs are warning the public to avoid charitable scams that fraudulently promise donations will go to victims of Hurricane Katrina.*

*The American Red Cross is now sheltering more than 159,000 hurricane survivors in 650 shelters spread across 17 states.*

With the addition of a hand sanitizer, insect repellant, and a sheet and light blanket, I completed my packing. The latter two items were a substitution I made for the sleeping bag included on the list. I couldn't imagine needing a sleeping bag, given that the likely nighttime temperatures would be in the 70's and 80's, and I assumed we wouldn't have air conditioning.

On this last evening together and anticipating how much I would miss my family, the otherwise routine activities of having dinner together, discussing the day's news, and helping the boys with homework took on additional significance and pleasure. They expressed their continued support for my leaving on this volunteer mission, and it felt great to have that encouragement. After pulling up the bed covers to my chin, I pondered my hopes and expectations for the upcoming two weeks. I made a self-promise that I would push myself to my absolute limit to do everything I could to make a difference, and that I would keep an open heart and mind about what I might encounter. I prayed to God that I would be empowered to do so.

# 2

## *To the Frontline*

*How wonderful it is that nobody need wait a single moment before starting to improve the world.*

*—Anne Frank*

**Friday, September 9**

*Admiral Timothy Keating, in charge of coordinating the military's response to Hurricane Katrina, said today that they never anticipated a scenario in which first responders and infrastructure were incapacitated. Along the Gulf Coast, Keating said, the infrastructure was wiped out, communications were nil, and roads and waterways were impassible.*

With it being a weekday, it was a business-like morning of getting breakfast and preparing for our days. With kisses and hugs goodbye, and a promise to talk by phone in the evening, Lisa, Dylan, and Austin left for work and school. I remained at home to take care of a few work-related emails and phone calls, then drove to a nearby hotel to catch the one and one-half hour shuttle to Denver International Airport. I arrived at about 10:30 a.m. for my scheduled 12:30 p.m. departure, with every minute of that two hours being needed. The Delta ticket agent informed me that he saw my reservation on his computer, but I had not yet been ticketed. I called the travel company, BTI, to find out what was going on. The explanation was that it was a two-step process, and that because of the huge number of Red Cross volunteers that they were processing, it had not yet been completed. The BTI representative told me that the specific staff person who made my reservation needed to do the ticketing and, as it turned out, there was currently a fire alarm going off in the building and that person had just gone outside. She explained that she would have the ticketing agent take care of it as soon as she returned. Pondering how it was that the person I was talking to didn't also need to go outside, I decided to let it go and not ask. About 30 minutes later (with only ten minutes to spare for being able to check luggage), she called back and told me the ticketing had been completed. The rest of the flight to Atlanta, where I changed planes, went without a hitch.

I had only been in the Atlanta International Airport two times before this trip, but I knew that there was usually a preponderance of gate changes. I didn't notice it at first because I usually tune out airport announcements. However, when I had been at this airport the last time, I began to pay more attention when I noticed that various flights were being changed from one gate to another. With so many messages that included the letters and numbers of gates, I fully expected someone to yell out "Bingo!" So, this time I paid close attention to the announcements, but the gate of my flight to Montgomery was not changed.

During that short flight I sat next to a pleasant fellow—a white man probably in his late 50's—who had lived all of his life in Montgomery. I mentioned something about the upcoming 50th anniversary of Rosa Park's role in the historic Montgomery bus boycott, which I had recently read about. We casually discussed several issues related to race relations, and his responses indicated that he was not prejudiced. I then made some comment about the racist treatment of blacks during the 1960's in the South, unwisely forgetting that I was now not only in the South, but that I was talking with a white Southerner whom I didn't know. "You know what? There were actually more blacks killed in race riots in Boston than in Montgomery," my seatmate tactfully but pointedly responded. I immediately knew that I had committed a social faux pas as a Yankee in the South. I resolved to think a bit more before speaking, now that I was a visitor.

Upon arrival at the baggage claim area in the Montgomery airport, I noticed a knot of about eight people gathering around a friendly-looking, bespectacled black man with a Red Cross vest on. Al introduced himself as our shuttle driver, a Red Cross volunteer, and from the Montgomery area. Males were under-represented within our group, with one other fellow who was a nurse. We quickly introduced ourselves to each other and told where we hailed from. All were from the eastern third of the country, with the exception of two women from Nebraska and San Francisco, and me. I would guess that all were younger than me, although one woman might have been close. It turned out that almost all of us shared the experience of being told by the ticket counter staff that we had reservations but weren't ticketed, necessitating urgent phone calls to remedy the situation. Our volunteer escort drove us in a van to the South Inn, a few miles from the airport, arriving at about 7:30 p.m. A second group of another eight or so Red Cross volunteers soon showed up in another van. The drive did not take long, as there was little traffic. Our route took us through a commercial/industrial neighborhood that was only marginally above the rundown-looking category. It was getting close to dusk, and the weather was short-sleeves comfortable, and overcast.

The lobby area of the South Inn looked perfectly acceptable to me, at least a one-diamond rating out of five, if the AAA were to rate it. However, as my newly-assigned roommate, Alan, and I proceeded down the hallway, the one diamond rating began to fade. By the time we entered the room and checked it out, anything resembling a precious gem to recognize this place would be a disservice to the rating system. The fragrance of cheap deodorizer was complemented by the unmistakable smell of mildew. My eyes were first drawn to the not-entirely-attached wallpaper border, which featured angels with pained facial expressions flying over pastoral New England landscapes as they blew their trumpets. The room did include the modern amenity of electrical outlets, but they were hanging loose out of the wall. I'm not the type of person who worries about contracting foot fungus from public showers, but I definitely regretted not bringing some flip-flop sandals when I saw that bathroom.

However, I wasn't worried about safety, and I saw humor in the setting. Ever since I spent a sleepless night a few decades ago in a cheap motel in India—where I needed to stuff my clothing under the door to keep the very persistent rats at bay—my tolerance for motels in the United States had increased appreciably. As long as it was quiet enough for a good night's sleep I would be happy. I also reminded myself that these accommodations would certainly be better than anything that I would encounter during the next two weeks.

Our group of eight had decided to meet back in the lobby before heading out for a bite to eat at a Shoney's Restaurant about one-half mile down the highway. Our short journey in the van was in the other direction from the airport, punctuated with a highway overpass, a few dark industrial buildings, and fast-food restaurants. I demonstrated my ignorance of the South and of chain restaurants by mentioning that I had never heard of Shoney's. Through a bit of research done later, I learned that there are 318 Shoney restaurants, not only in the South but also in much of the East, effectively putting one in every reasonably-sized city within those regions.

During a two-week family vacation to the South Carolina and Georgia coast the previous March, I had become completely enamored with Southern cooking: barbequed chicken, sweet potatoes, corn bread, fried okra, collard greens, pecan pie…you get the idea. I must have been spoiled by going to independently-operated and highly-recommended restaurants in Charleston and Savannah, because the chicken-fried steak and salad didn't come close to the food that I still recalled with a salivation response. Our table of six ordered a side of fried dill pickles to share, but there was more humor gained from them than eating pleasure.

A good portion of the conversation at our table was dominated by two of our members sharing sarcastic comments about the inhospitable conditions of the South Inn. While recognizing the social and bonding value of shared complaining for a group of strangers, I soon grew weary of it. Part of me wanted to remind them that this was a *hardship* deployment, and if they expected the Ramada Inn, they would be in for a very rude awakening when we reached our shelters. However, that would only be complaining about their complaining, so instead of ostracizing myself, I politely departed and went out to wait for the shuttle to take us back to the motel. Upon discovering that some of the other Red Cross volunteers had already been waiting about 15 minutes for the shuttle, I decided I would walk back. I happened to notice that Carrie, one of the volunteers, had also just exited the restaurant. Maybe in her young 40's, Carrie had shoulder-length brown hair, and was about 5' 7" tall. From previous casual conversation, something about her made me feel that she was a kindred spirit. I invited her to join me for the walk back and she readily accepted. My perception of her was affirmed when she shared my sentiments of seeing irony and being a bit disgruntled by the prissy comments about the lodging. Realizing that we both had traveled to India, we shared some stories about our experiences. Carrie told me that she worked as a nurse at a hospital in San Francisco and that she had paid for her own travel expenses flying to Alabama. From our conversation, I found Carrie to be intelligent and compassionate, and it was reaffirming to know that we were on the same "team."

Alan and I arrived back at our room at about the same time. A young psychologist from Canton, Ohio, he had a quick smile about him. He would be assisting with the mental health portion of the relief effort, having responded to an appeal by the American Psychological Association. As we got ready for sleep, Alan pondered out loud, "Maybe I should take some Claritin."

"What are you allergic to?" I asked.

"Mold and mildew, for starters," Alan responded.

"I have the impression there's some of that around," I said. For whatever reason, however, he eventually decided against it. Within another hour, I greatly regretted not jumping at the chance to encourage him with all of my persuasive skills to take that medication. A bit of background information is needed here. I apparently have a very bad karma thing going when it comes to getting roommates highly skilled at snoring. By all indications, the Supreme Being feels that I have some issues to resolve around tolerating snoring roommates. Over the course of the past 20 years, I have probably been in 30 different situations of sharing sleeping accommodations with men in motels, hotels, cabins, hostels, yurts, tents and campers. Every time, and I mean *every* time, at least one of the guys in the group has snored loudly enough to completely defy any earplugs commercially available.

Just as I was about to fall asleep, Alan began his snoring. It started out as a wispy sort of thing with each inhalation. It soon evolved into more of a guttural sound. I tried to humor myself by thinking of how to spell the sound he was making, but I gave up. I didn't want to be unkind to this near-stranger by waking him, but I had to do something. I thought if I sort of quickly yelled his name while still pretending to be asleep, it might wake him up without his really knowing what awakened him. He then might roll into another sleeping position, other than on his back, and stop the snoring. I yelled his name, a mild yell at first, but that did nothing. I gradually increased the volume, and still he slept like a rock. I ended up yelling his name so loud that I thought I would wake up the next door neighbors, and still Alan peacefully snored and slept. It was time for Plan B. My bed was closest to the outside wall, near the air conditioner. My ingenious idea was to crank up the air conditioner to the highest level, thinking that it would benefit in two ways. First, it would help to drown out the sound of the snoring, and second, it would make the room so cold that he would roll off of his back and into a fetal position for warmth. I implemented the plan and smugly congratulated myself for my creative thinking.

Thirty minutes later, I was still awake and was getting cold. The white noise of the air conditioner helped some, but not completely. Looking over at Alan, I saw that he was still blissfully sleeping on his back, sawing logs to his heart's content. With only a sheet for a cover, he showed no indication of being cold. I pulled my blanket and bedspread over my head, assumed a fetal position and eventually fell asleep.

## Saturday, September 10

*During the previous ten days, images and stories from New Orleans of looting, mayhem, alleged rapes in the Superdome, and a shot fired at a rescue helicopter have been imprinted into the brains of most Americans through television news and newspaper articles. Many people have found that to be one of the most dispiriting aspects of the tragedy. However, a Boston Globe article today reported that, in fact, no shot was ever fired at a rescue helicopter and there was only one averted rape attempt in the Superdome. Many experts on disaster aftermaths and crowd behavior believe that much of that violent impression was created in large part by rumor and amplified by gullible reporters. The scholars' suspicions were fueled by what they said is a well-documented history of misinformation during disasters—and a general human tendency to mis-read crowds as more malevolent than they really are.*

By 7:00 a.m., most of the Red Cross volunteers had congregated in the motel lobby, waiting for the shuttles to take us to the Montgomery Red Cross headquarters. The motel was offering a hot breakfast, but it was handled by placing your order with an employee at the reception desk, who then walked into the back room, where there was presumably a rudimentary kitchen facility. Because the breakfast orders were being cranked out at the pace of about one order per 10 minutes and at least 16 people were milling about, my math calculations and sense of urgency sent me back to my room for a quick bowl of granola.

I was part of the first shuttle group that left around 7:30 a.m., and we quickly arrived at the headquarters building a few miles away. As we had been informed previously by the recording, the headquarters was housed in what used to be a K-Mart. It must have been on the market in a somewhat abandoned condition when the Red Cross arranged to utilize the premises.

In the coming weeks, there would be seven or eight scenes in which I would have a dramatic and instantaneous sense of the vast scale of the hurricane. Driving into the parking lot, then walking into the headquarters building, were my first two. The large parking lot, typical-sized for a K-Mart, was three-fourths filled with vehicles, almost all of them being small to medium size rental trucks, such as from Budget and Penske, with Red Cross placards on them. These were just the Red Cross vehicles that were there, ready for deployment. Who knows, I thought, probably five times that many were already being used for deliveries between Montgomery and the Mississippi and Alabama coasts. Then I recalled that there was also a similar, even larger relief effort going on in the Baton Rouge/New Orleans area.

When I walked into the building, I was again startled with a better comprehension of the scope of Katrina's impact. It was a conventional K-Mart building, but instead of it having aisles and aisles of consumer goods, it was filled with hundreds of scurrying people (some who looked like they knew what they were doing, and many who didn't), communications and computer equipment, tables being staffed, maps, dry-erase boards with information, boxes of supplies, and cordoned-off areas with people at desks and on phones. An astonishing and very palpable sense of adrenaline-charged urgency made it feel like the floor of the New York Stock Exchange. Some of the people had been in a "crisis mode" for almost two weeks and were understandably quite stressed, sleep-deprived, and on edge. Others, like me, were rookies with a mixed bag of enthusiasm, excitement, and anxiety.

We followed yelled-out directions to dump our luggage in a certain area and to go to a nearby space where we would be given a pre-orientation. This consisted of on-the-fly instructions from a volunteer—recently assigned as a trainer—informing us about how to fill out more forms. She quickly told us about the remaining steps needed: another orientation presentation, checking in at the health desk, obtaining a debit card at another desk, and then proceeding to a work area (mine being Shelter Operations) to wait for an assignment. At the health desk I was asked several questions, given a few handout sheets, and reminded to wash my hands *often*. At the financial desk I learned that they had run out of the Red Cross debit cards, but might be handing out cash advances in another hour. The card or the money would be used for pre-approved expenses, such as meals and lodging if needed.

The primary orientation meeting was given by the man who was currently in charge of this headquarters operation. Don was a retiree from New Hampshire with a sense of humor and a very forthright manner. Immediately, he admitted to the situation being extremely chaotic, frenetic, and seemingly disorganized. In the same breath, he defended what was happening as a function of it being an unprecedented disaster with literally each minute bringing a new reality with which to deal, and staffed almost entirely by barely-trained volunteers. By means of a combination of his words and his direct and persuasive style, he convinced me—at least for the moment. Don also genuinely expressed the importance of upholding and demonstrating the Red Cross principles, particularly the importance of being sensitive and considerate of the people that we would be serving, whom we should refer to as our clients. The most memorable thing that he said was, with this being such an extreme disaster, that we might need to "throw out the rule book and base our decisions on good judgment instead." "And," he continued, "if you think that you probably shouldn't do something that might be questionable ethically or morally, then don't do it." I would end up basing more than a few decisions on those two sentences of advice.

By this point, the original group of volunteers from the motel had scattered throughout the large floor area, dispersed among the hundreds of people. We were on our own unless we happened to have "palled up" in some smaller unit. Since the assignments entailed a wide assortment of jobs, to many dozens of locations in Alabama and Mississippi, it seemed logical that I might not see the members of the original group again, after leaving this headquarters. I realized that if I felt that I might want to communicate with a volunteer at a future point, I should get their contact information as soon as possible, since we could part ways with little, if any, warning. Of the two volunteers that I had the most interest in maintaining contact, I did not see Alan again, but I did cross paths with Carrie at a later time.

I went to the Shelter Operations area and learned that a few of the volunteers had been waiting for a couple of days for an assignment, having even slept there overnight on cots under the buzzing glow of the fluorescent lights. With nothing happening, I returned to the financial desk where there was a long line of people waiting for their advance money, which the staff now had. The woman administering the process was clearly over the edge with stress and frustration. With a flushed face and clenched teeth, she screamed at the top of her voice, "Read the signs! We have three lines here, according to the first letter of your last name!" Remarkably, there was so much background activity and noise that her loud and emotional voice drew little attention. After standing in the line for ten minutes, I learned that the money was only being distributed to people who had been waiting since the day before.

I went back to the Shelter Operations area, soon to be enlivened by a woman running up and announcing to all within hearing range that she urgently needed about 60 people to go to the Gulfport area. This request caused a real stir in the crowd, as people quickly gathered around her to hear more. She explained that four shelters in Gulfport needed to be re-staffed. This statement got my immediate interest, because Gulfport was one of the Mississippi coast towns hardest hit. She was joined by a man who apparently had the assignment of lining up the managers for these shelters, and he thought that four groups of two would be good. "How many people here have experience at managing a Red Cross shelter?" he asked, looking for a show of hands. Only one person out of about 60 responded. Undeterred, he followed up by asking "Okay, how many have transferable skills, like with managing a business or leading a group of people?" While I hesitated and thought about it, four or five people raised their hands. A 15-second interview of each was conducted, and I moved closer to hear their responses. Concluding that they all had apparently passed their tests, I reflected on my skills and experience relative to what they had described, thought it over for about five seconds, and boldly stepped forward to offer my services. I presented a two-sentence summary of my experience at managing people and finances, he looked me up and down, and said, "Okay, you team up with him," pointing at the gentleman who was the sole one with actual experience at running a Red Cross shelter. And with that, I was blessed and sanctified as a Red Cross shelter manager, and the specific path of my Red Cross experience became much more defined.

I was now beginning to get a feel for how this all worked. If I had sat down and waited for someone to walk up to me individually to give me an assignment, I would likely have spent my entire two weeks in what used to be the lingerie section of a K-Mart. On the other hand, by taking some initiative and expressing confidence, I could guide the nature of my experience much more. If I had desired, I probably could have talked my way into either being a delivery driver or staying at the Montgomery headquarters to assist with numerous tasks there. I was beside myself with excitement over this assignment. It's exactly what I had hoped.

There wasn't more than a minute to gloat over my good fortune, though, as George, my co-manager, suggested that I photocopy the Shelter Management Handbook that he had just scrounged from somewhere. It was less than an hour before we would leave, and we had to gather all of the materials that might be needed. I laboriously photocopied the 60-page bound manual, page by page, with the machine running out of paper and becoming jammed several times. I went over to the shelter office supplies desk, and quickly loaded up a box of everything available, such as pens, paper, stapler, paper clips, and masking tape. It was as if I won a contest and had 60 seconds to decadently load up my box with whatever I wanted.

The eight of us newly-anointed shelter managers walked outside to load up with our driver into our white Ford van and began the four and one-half hour drive to Gulfport. The temperature was comfortably warm and the skies partly cloudy. Our route included traveling the highway walked by thousands during the historic Selma to Montgomery march in 1965. I reflected upon that event, but our primary focus was obviously upon preparing ourselves for our upcoming duties. We handed around the photocopied Shelter Management Handbook in sections while getting to know each other and discussing what we might expect and how to handle it. Although I did read most of the material, it all seemed to be common sense stuff related to setting up and operating a shelter. One of our group, Carl, was exceedingly studious about this training opportunity, taking copious notes from the photocopies. Good-natured ribbing predictably came at his expense. A pleasant, thirty-something married couple, Ted and Susan, lived in Charlotte, North Carolina. Ben was employed by the Peace Corps national headquarters in Washington D.C., having completed a Peace Corps assignment in Africa. Our group also included a curious fellow with a very thick rural North Carolina accent, who apparently was a very accomplished kick boxer. I would later think that we could have used him for security, but I heard that he was "let go" for some mysterious reason.

A few things we observed during our drive down:

- Gas prices were surprisingly low at about $2.60 per gallon, as compared with at least $3.00 per gallon elsewhere in the country.

- We noticed on a number of occasions convoys of trucks and other vehicles from light and power utilities from several northern states headed in the same direction as us towards the gulf coast. This heightened the sense of reality about what we were headed towards.

- There was a proliferation of an insect that locals call love bugs. These insects were seen in one of two ways: either flying around in copulatory bliss, joined rear end to rear end, or smeared into a black mass on every vehicle's windshield and front bumper.

- We began to see blown-down highway signs and downed trees in Selma, gradually increasing in number as we drove through the towns of Meridian, Hattiesburg, and eventually Gulfport.

- In Meridian and Hattiesburg we also started to see an increasing frequency of damaged roofs, apparent more due to blue tarps on the roofs rather than visible damage. The blue tarps were well-known to the members of our group who had previously experienced hurricanes, as it is part of a Federal Emergency Management Agency (FEMA) program to temporarily protect homes before the roofs can be repaired.

"Love bugs" smeared on a car's front grill and bumper

We arrived in Gulfport about 6:00 p.m. With a population of around 75,000, it is surprising that it is the second largest city in Mississippi, after the capital of Jackson. Prior to the hurricane, Gulfport was known for its legalized gambling on casinos moored on the beachfront; an attractive, restored downtown; being a base of operations for shrimp boats; and its several military bases in the immediate area, including a U.S. Navy Seabee base. Hurricane Katrina effectively removed from the map the first two of those four elements, and dealt a blow to the latter two.

The Gulfport Red Cross headquarters was located in an industrial-looking building about five miles from the coast, so there wasn't a tremendous amount of structural damage in that area. It was too late to be able to do much that day, so we were directed to the Three Rivers Elementary School about two miles away for sleeping. We were to report back with our luggage the next morning at 7:30 a.m. for further instructions. The school was abuzz with hundreds of Red Cross volunteers, with cots spread out in the hallways and gym/lunchroom. I happened to see Carrie, the nurse from San Francisco who was part of my original group in Montgomery. She had arrived earlier with her medical team, which had been assembled back in Montgomery. I set up a cot near her down one of the hallways, as she had already scoped it out as being less congested and with cooler temperatures. She and I went for a short walk in our immediate neighborhood, which included an impromptu tent city set up in the adjacent baseball field complex that was occupied by volunteer utility workers from around the country. It was enjoyable spending time with Carrie and getting to know her better.

Before going to sleep I peeked inside one of the classrooms that happened to be for fifth grade. I was touched by photographs of the children and their art work and essays posted on the walls. It reminded me of my fifth grade son, Austin. It was as if I were seeing a photograph of their normal lives frozen in time, just before the hurricane hit. I wondered where they were living now, if they had evacuated Gulfport and if their homes had suffered much damage. God forbid that any of them might have perished. This disaster was becoming much more tangible.

## Sunday, September 11

*President Bush returned today to the Gulf Coast for an overnight stay as workers continued to crisscross the receding flood waters of New Orleans in search of bodies. The Louisiana death toll stands at 197 and the national death toll at 429, but those numbers will climb as workers gain access to those who perished in their homes, and below the fetid water that continues to be pumped out of New Orleans. Several thousand residents remain in the wrecked city, and though there had been talk of removing them by force, that has not happened.*

I woke up about 6:30 a.m. with anticipation and excitement in knowing that this would be the first day to really acquire a sense of what I'd gotten myself into. I ate a quick breakfast (yes, my home-made granola), packed up my gear and proceeded outside where a few others in our group were gathering. George was standing outside, so we took the opportunity to get to know each other better and chat about our rapidly-approaching shelter management duty. I had learned the day before that George was a retired vice president of Blue Cross/Blue Shield for the New Hampshire and Vermont region and that he had previous experience as a Red Cross shelter manager. He wore glasses and had graying and thinning hair that was covered with a beige crushable cotton hat. George was wearing a light-colored tee-shirt under his Red Cross vest and light-colored shorts, which would be his standard dress for our time together. George impressed me as having a nice blend of forthrightness—perhaps honed by his New England environment and business manager background—and a grandfatherly warm heart. Similarly, I later observed that as a manager George was typically decisive, but could still be flexible when it came to accepting the structure and bureaucracy of the Red Cross. I suspected that his many years of working as a manager with a large corporation fostered those characteristics.

I began our conversation by saying, "George, my first executive decision as a shelter co-manager is to appoint you as the manager and myself as the assistant manager." In my opinion, the co-manager idea was destined to create confusion between ourselves, our staff members and the clients, as to who was responsible for what. He was clearly the better choice for the top dog role, from his business management and Red Cross experience. The bottom line was that we needed to complete as much work as efficiently as possible, and it was perfectly fine with me to function as an assistant manager and do whatever needed to be done in that role. He diplomatically and genuinely responded that it didn't really matter to him which way we did it, but I emphatically held my ground.

While talking with George and waiting for a driver and a vehicle to take us to Red Cross headquarters I kept an eye open for Carrie. I had regretted not getting Alan's contact information—or even his last name—and I didn't want to make that mistake with Carrie. However, a driver soon drove up and asked if we needed a ride, and we needed to take advantage of the opportunity.

When entering the headquarters after the short two-mile drive, I was again impressed with the feeling of high energy and crisis-mode ambiance. One large room—about the size of a tennis court—was now occupied with all manner of tables, maps, computers, boxes of supplies, and perhaps 100 Red Cross personnel darting around, engaged in various tasks, and in dozens of noisy conversations. It was very loud when I first entered, and after being there a short while, I had the sense that it was becoming even more so. It was as if every person engaged in one of the many conversations couldn't quite hear, so they escalated their voice, resulting in an ever-increasing din.

It would end up being a few more hours before the appropriate Red Cross staff would be able to gather all of the necessary information to make the decisions about who would be going to which shelter. While waiting, George and I did our best to prepare ourselves by picking up handout information, listening in on various conversations, and networking.

We had heard an announcement the evening before that there was going to be a brief service at 9:00 a.m. this morning, September 11th, in recognition of the lives lost and heroic acts associated with the 9/11 tragedy four years ago. As that time approached, I noticed the preparation that was taking place on the small stage off to the side of the room. The vast majority of the people in the room were oblivious to or only mildly aware of it, being so engaged in their own urgent tasks. My attention was drawn to six men on the stage, identified with their blue t-shirts and/or ball caps as New York City firefighters. One of them was holding an American flag on a short pole, and they were beginning to line themselves up. I had noticed a few of them from the evening before and had correctly guessed that they were down here volunteering with the relief effort. My eyes were especially drawn to one of those six, who was mustached, maybe 55 years old, on the short side and with a fire-hydrant build (appropriately so). I could tell that he was anticipating the emotional difficulty of the upcoming service. He was swallowing hard and tightening the muscles of his face, trying to steel himself. I felt a pang of sadness and compassion well up in me, imagining the grim memories and grief that he was experiencing.

Right at 9:00 a.m., a Red Cross chaplain spoke into a microphone, asking for the attention of the audience. The reverence and respect for the event was evident by the immediate and absolute quieting of the crowd, from near-deafening noise to absolute silence, and I mean *absolute* silence. The chaplain began with an eloquent prayer, honoring the thousands of lives that were lost in New York City, Washington D.C., and Pennsylvania and expressing appreciation for the great sacrifices and heroic acts of the New York City firefighters and police officers.

After the prayer, he asked the audience to express its gratitude and respect for the firefighters on the stage. The applause and cheers were, as you would expect, loud and heartfelt, then grew in intensity and emotional expression and became even louder. The firemen were clearly appreciative. A few nodded, and they became fidgety with the attention they were receiving and their own emotions. The chaplain held up a hand to quiet the crowd, then tactfully and appropriately said, "These guys are obviously appreciative of your support, but it's becoming too much for them." The firefighter previously described was now very overcome, and his comrades on both sides of him and behind him laid their hands on his shoulders to bolster him. One of the other firemen spoke up to express their group's deep respect and appreciation for the thousands of Red Cross volunteers and citizens who supported them through the tragedy. The chaplain said a few closing words, and with that, the ten-minute service was over. As people wiped tears from their eyes, they turned back to their business at hand, and the adrenalinized energy and noise returned to the previous level.

Soon thereafter, George and I learned that we were being assigned to a shelter at Gulfport Central Elementary School. We would be joined by two Red Cross volunteers, Dawn and Frank, whom we had recently met. Dawn and Frank both appeared to be in their early to mid-30's and wore glasses. Dawn had long brown hair and was of average height. I would later learn that she lived in the Seattle area, worked as a legal secretary, possessed a warm heart, an ability to read people, and a great laugh. Frank worked as a programmer/analyst for a utility department on the East Coast. He sported short black hair and a serious demeanor that partially masked his compassion and dry sense of humor.

While the chaotic assignment of other managers to shelters ensued, I took note of the dry-erase board mounted on the wall behind the table. I saw the Gulfport Central Elementary School listed second out of about 15 shelters, with various bits of information, including the facts that they had 90 clients the night before and that they had a need for five nurses. I wondered why they would need so many nurses. While other assignments were being made, I overheard that one of the other Gulfport shelters had been visited recently by Barbara Walters and some other celebrity.

Shelter-planning board at Gulfport Red Cross headquarters

Prior to leaving, all of us soon-to-be shelter managers received a ten-minute orientation/pep talk outside. The only thing I recall is the trainer laughing long and hard about a previous orientation she had given, in which the manager-to-be had asked which motel she would be staying in.

George, Dawn, Frank, and I then hopped in a Red Cross van with our gear and proceeded to the school that would serve as our shelter. It was about five miles away. As we turned off Highway 49 onto Pass Road, I could see a National Guard checkpoint ahead, limiting the traffic that could proceed beyond that point towards downtown and the coast. As we got closer to the school, we noticed an increasing number of billboard-sized signs and poles blown over, along with trees and tree limbs. Most of the standing trees were void of leaves, giving an eerie feeling of dormancy in September. Many traffic lights were down, including the wires overhead that had supported them. These intersections were being treated as four-way stops, which made for a dangerous situation. The local people knew at which intersections there had previously been a traffic light, but outsiders wouldn't unless they were very observant.

As we turned into the school, I noticed that it had the appearance of a typical one-story brick elementary school, with a few exceptions. An incredibly large pile of trash sprawled across the alley, and a monstrous roll-off dumpster and about 16 Porta-Toilets were placed in the asphalt parking lot. The front steps and the entry area were protected from the sun and rain by a good-sized overhang. This same overhang continued down the length of the front of the building and out for ten feet to cover a concrete walkway. The ground of the entire front area was covered by either asphalt or concrete, save for a twenty-foot diameter circle within which grew a large and stately oak tree. Katrina had apparently stripped its leaves and many of its smaller branches, some of which were piled in a scattered manner at its base. This landscaped island also featured the obligatory flagpole, at that time holding a limp American flag.

About 15 adults were lounging around the front of the school—primarily under the overhang—sitting on the front steps, eight or nine well-used, child-sized chairs, and an ugly old sofa such as one might see in front of a college student rental property. A few people were in their easily-identified red and white Red Cross vests, the others I assumed to be clients.

We introduced ourselves at the crudely set up registration table and were directed to the office of the current manager, Jill. She had short brown hair and was about 5' 8" tall. I would have guessed her to be about 40, but after hearing what she had been through, she might have easily been younger than that, with the extra years being a temporary feature due to stress and chronic sleep deprivation. She gave the impression of being a very in-charge person, hard-wired to overcome con-current crises. I later observed that her sturdy and assertive exterior was coupled with a compassionate heart.

Over the next few days of our overlap in duty—and in brief snatches of time while simultaneously dealing with countless issues and problems—Jill filled us in on the two-week history of the shelter, including her tenure as manager. This information turned out to be invaluable in dealing with the problems that we would encounter. It helped immensely in understanding the preceding factors and conditions under which most of the current clients had survived. It helped to explain and justify the clients' extreme range and intensity of emotions that we would be observing and need to deal with over the next ten days. Lastly, it was of great benefit to hear Jill's insights on the clients themselves: who was helpful and trustworthy, who had medical problems that needed attention, who were the potential trouble-makers, etc.

As she told it—and based upon what she had heard from the clients and two Red Cross predecessors—on Sunday, August 28th, the day before the hurricane hit, about 180 people from the surrounding neighborhood gradually gathered at the school, seeking refuge in it as a spontaneous shelter. The vast majority of these people were living below the poverty line, and about half were homeless. Most did not own a vehicle, and if they did they could not afford the cost of a motel room. Nor was there the option to evacuate to a safe haven at a relative's home, due to having limited or strained relationships with family. The custodian had unlocked the building for their use, but there was no management or leadership of it as a shelter at that point, whether from the school district, the local police, the Red Cross, or any other agency.

These people weathered the hurricane itself all right, in terms of physical damage to the building, but numerous, grim problems soon developed. The first two Red Cross volunteers showed up two days after the hurricane, with Jill and another Red Cross volunteer arriving two days later. Although Jill had not previously managed a Red Cross shelter, she did have substantial experience with managing a domestic violence and sexual assault shelter in Virginia, along with previous experience as an Emergency Medical Technician. She would use all of those skills—and then some—over the next few weeks. Initially deployed as a shelter care volunteer, she ended up being reassigned in temporary health services because there was a shortage of nurses. After three days at the shelter, effectively serving many of the managerial duties, she was officially designated as its manager.

By the time Jill had come on the scene, the shelter did have bottled water and Meals Ready to Eat (M.R.E.'s). She was not sure how long the shelter residents had gone without food and water. With her first assessment, the prioritized problems were health services, sanitation, and security, in that order. None of the utilities were working—electricity, water, or sewer—but the shelter did have one generator, with a limited amount of gas to run it.

Jill and the other Red Cross volunteer who arrived with her had hit the ground running, immediately determining the prioritized medical needs and addressing them as well. They worked until 3:30 a.m. the next morning, got one and one-half hours of sleep, and started again. Medical supplies were very limited—most of them came from the staff's personal first aid kits—so there was little they could do to resolve the major health concerns. For example, there were numerous diabetic clients, but there were no glucometers to check their blood sugar, nor was there any insulin. Many people were critically dependent upon certain medications (for heart conditions, high blood pressure, chronic mental health problems, seizures, and HIV), but they had exhausted whatever amounts they had brought with them. For the first few days there was only one hospital open in the Gulfport/Biloxi area. That hospital was triaging and would only take near-death cases.

Several life-threatening situations during Jill's tenure added to the stress. One such case involved a client with severe high blood pressure and no medication. Although the staff did not have a blood pressure cuff to monitor him, they knew that he was exhibiting pre-stroke signs and symptoms, exacerbated by the heat and emotional stress. No vehicle or gas was available to transport him. Eventually, they procured another client's vehicle with an empty gas tank, filled it with a few precious gallons of gas from the limited supply being used for the generator, and took him to the local hospital, with no guarantee that the hospital staff would be willing to see him. (Fortunately, they did.) A second client with major heart problems was rushed to the emergency room. Yet another was dehydrated and had gastrointestinal problems thought to be due to eating spoiled meat from a refrigerator that had lost power days earlier. A rescue squad from Georgia that was supposed to have left town hours earlier to head home stayed around long enough to hang an intravenous fluid drip on him. Lacking the conventional equipment, the IV bag was duct-taped to the wall.

Jill's list went on. A woman was suffering from a gangrenous toe and a male client was afflicted with necrotic tissue (the skin was sloughing off) from an untreated spider bite to his elbow. A pregnant woman was sent to the hospital via rescue squad when she reached the point of being very dilated. The emergency room sent her back with the advice to return when the baby's head was "crowning." The rescue squad gave the staff a childbirth kit from their ambulance, just in case it was needed. The client eventually left the shelter without giving birth.

Jill felt that most of what she and her staff were able to provide to the clients during the first couple of days was comfort and reassurance. It gave them the sense that a person with some medical knowledge was taking charge, that their conditions were being closely monitored, and that they were being cared for as well as could be expected under the circumstances.

Some of the medical problems included criminal and mental health components. During Jill's first night there was an alleged rape. Since the Emergency Room was only processing life-threatening cases, there was no way to gather medical evidence. Lacking that or a witness, the police were unable to arrest the alleged perpetrator. The alleged victim was given a medical exam by an ambulance crew, and she was provided with rape crisis counseling by Jill. A Red Cross mental health worker was called in to consult and provide support, and the alleged perpetrator was evicted from the shelter. With this problem occurring in such an environment—with the magnitude of the disaster and the lack of resources—there was nothing else that could be done.

Over the course of the next several days, medical conditions had gradually improved. By Sunday, September 4th, Red Cross nurses began arriving and the medical staff continued to strengthen. More medical supplies were delivered, pharmacies in the community started to reopen, and medication refills were given if the clients had their original prescription bottles. A walk-in clinic opened at the emergency room, and mobile medical teams with doctors and medications started showing up in the shelter's parking lot.

Although the medical conditions were gradually improving, the sanitation issue deteriorated to the point of near-crisis. With no running water and no Porta-Toilets, the clients continued to use the bathroom facilities, occasionally flushing them with water from a nearby creek—but not often enough. (The water was being hauled in large drums in the back of a pick-up truck, from a creek a mile or so away. The shortage of gas and labor limited the frequency of those trips.) The fecal material from some of the overflowing toilets was inadvertently tracked out from the bathroom floors to the school's hallways. It was not only a problem of a repulsive lack of sanitation but also was a potentially serious health issue. Jill and her staff did all that they could to try to resolve the problem. Some AmeriCorp volunteers showed up and worked to clean and sanitize everything in sight with bleach. With every agency that came through the front door (and there were many), Jill informed them of the urgency of getting Porta-Toilets delivered.

Eventually, on Sunday, September 4th, still without running water for indoor toilets or any Porta-Toilets outside, the Mississippi Department of Health decided they would need to shut the shelter down because of the risk of infectious disease. Several buses pulled up in the school's parking lot with the intent of relocating the clients to another shelter. With that news, the clients became very upset because many of them had recently secured jobs doing hurricane clean-up work within walking distance. Being relocated to a more distant shelter would result in a loss of their jobs. They were able to persuade the agency to give them another day, and that turned out to be enough. The next day, Monday—one week after the hurricane's landfall—16 Porta-Toilets were delivered to the school parking lot. Jill later discovered that the Gulfport Police chief had "gone to bat" for the shelter, pulling whatever strings were necessary to have the Porta-Toilets delivered and averting the need to close it. The Porta-Toilets enabled the cordoning off of the bathrooms so that they could be thoroughly sterilized by a contract company that specialized in such clean-up. Several days later, on September 7th, water service was restored, although it was considered non-potable.

The third primary problem area for Jill and her staff had been security. When Jill arrived, two Gulfport police officers were assigned to the shelter, each working a 12-

hour shift and having had little, if any, time off since the hurricane hit. In Jill's opinion, they were doing an incredible job and were of great support to her, even though both of their homes had been destroyed, and they were separated from their families who had been evacuated elsewhere. Still, it was a potentially volatile situation, given more than 120 people being on edge with stressful conditions, and some of them without their prescribed psychotropic medications. It was hot and humid—even during the night—so the clients would leave doors open for ventilation, and some would sleep outside. No shelter curfew had been established, and people would come and go as they pleased.

Within a few days of arriving, Jill and her staff had implemented standard Red Cross shelter procedures with regard to security. A curfew was imposed, and a front desk was set up with check-in and check-out procedures. Shelter rules were posted and enforced, and designated staff members made security rounds at night. After the electricity was restored on September 5th, they were able to run the air conditioning, thus lessening the desire to leave doors open for ventilation (although not completely, since the air conditioner was a swamp cooler with a leak in its water reservoir). The sense of security and control of activities further improved as the Red Cross staff gradually grew from four at Jill's arrival, to 14 or 15 by the time that we arrived.

Midway during Jill's first week, security consultants from the Red Cross national headquarters arrived to discuss more advanced security issues not covered in the standard Red Cross training. For example, the clients were prohibited from having weapons, but neither the Red Cross nor the police could legally search a client without probable cause or other justification. Furthermore, what exactly defines a "weapon"? Is a hammer or a screwdriver a weapon? Some of the clients owned such tools—needed for their jobs—and were without a vehicle to store them in. The security consultants also provided recommendations for contingency plans in case a situation exceeded the abilities of the police officer and the Red Cross staff to handle it (for example, calling in the National Guard).

On at least one occasion of relating these stories to George and me, Jill caught herself mid-sentence, realizing that her words might be interpreted as portraying the clients in too negative a light. She made the point that most of the clients were cooperative, helpful, and kept trying to make the best of a very bad situation.

From Jill's previous experience with managing a domestic violence and sexual assault shelter and working as an EMT, she was used to being in crisis mode and "putting Band-Aids on bullet wounds." That phrase proved to be an apt description for her 20-hour work days managing this shelter prior to our arrival. As if that were not enough, she was also concerned about her personal health (although there was little time for that to enter her mind). On her third night at the shelter, Jill was holding a flashlight to assist a diabetic client in pricking her finger with a lancet so that her blood sugar could be tested. (They had finally gotten a glucometer, and she was the first client to use it.) Due to the poor light, Jill suffered an accidental needle-stick in her finger. The client informed Jill that she "had hepatitis, but not the contagious kind." With the client not able to provide more specific information, Jill was left to ponder the possibilities. She briefly considered that it might be hepatitis B, but was reassured in knowing that she had received a hepatitis B vaccination, as had all health care workers. She figured there was a small chance that it was hepatitis C, which is contagious, with no cure, and potentially fatal. If it did turn out that the woman had hepatitis C, and Jill had become infected, there would be tragic irony to it. A few years previous, Jill had donated a lobe of her liver to a friend who needed the liver transplant as a result of having hepatitis C. Jill reasoned, however, that the most probable circumstance was that the client had alcoholic hepatitis, which is not contagious.

Still, it was clearly a situation that justified concern and the need for follow-up blood tests. With Jill's medical background, she knew that it was important to have it checked out, but at the time she was telling me this story—a full week after that incident—she had not yet made it to the hospital for the lab work. For the first few days, it had been difficult to arrange transportation to the hospital. The primary reason, though, was that there always seemed to be more pressing problems to resolve. Jill told this story to me with no hint of soliciting sympathy or playing the part of a martyr. It was all matter-of-fact, merely offering a synopsis of the many trials and tribulations. To put it mildly, I was quite impressed with her tireless, selfless, and courageous approach. A few days later Jill would leave for home, still not having made it to the hospital for the blood tests.

At that point, it would be fair to say that I was overwhelmed with what I had walked into and the standard set by our predecessor. In reality, we were confronted with two layers of challenge to manage this particular shelter. There was the expected set of obstacles to overcome in operating a shelter for people displaced by a hurricane. In addition, however, this particular population would add its own unique array of trials. I did feel extremely fortunate that I not only had another person to help me with the management of this shelter, but also that it happened to be a person who had had previous experience in doing so. On a few occasions George told people that it was taking two men to replace the work of one woman. He said it in a joking manner, but we both knew how very true that was.

From Jill's perspective, the current condition of the shelter and the clients within it was a Hilton Inn relative to what she first encountered nine days earlier.

From my perspective, the current condition was hardly comfy, clean, and secure, with plenty of reminders that a Category 4 hurricane had hit this area a scant 13 days before. In our first walk-through, I observed the following: although some of the clients had their belongings stashed orderly in boxes or bags under or near their cots, most had their stuff spread out all around them, including dirty laundry, trash, and half-eaten food. Even though the air conditioning was working for the auditorium, the hallways—where about two-thirds of the clients slept—were very warm, if not hot, despite several fans running. The bathrooms had overflowing trash cans and clothing thrown about. On the floor of the toilet stall was a disgusting-looking rag that had been used as a substitute for toilet paper. One of the bathrooms reeked so much that whenever I entered I would force myself to breathe out of my mouth rather than nose. The shower facilities for these 90 clients and 20 staff members consisted of one crudely constructed shower for each gender. The shower "stall" was made of black plastic attached to the wall and a toilet stall. It drained to the floor drain, which was clogged with a few wash clothes and various sizes and colors of bar soap. The water supply was a garden hose run to a hose bib. The water was unheated and still considered non-potable, so you had to make sure not to get it in your mouth, eyes, nose, or open wounds.

Still, while sensing that this experience was going to be emotionally challenging, I felt confident that I could deal with the physical hardships and less than sanitary conditions. Heck, there was enough Purell hand sanitizer around to kill every germ in the Center for Disease Control laboratories. Everywhere you looked there were bottles of it—on the bathroom sinks, on every food-distributing table, taped to stairway railings, and in the pockets of most Red Cross volunteers. (Investor tip: Buy lots of Purell stock a few days before the next major hurricane is predicted to hit the U.S.)

Over the course of this first day in the shelter, I met about 15 members of the Red Cross staff, with a few being on their off-day or occupied elsewhere. They had been at this shelter for anywhere between two days and two weeks. A large medical presence was evident, with a nurse's room set up, conveniently enough, in the school nurse's room. Our shelter was apparently being set up as a sort of triage center to handle a wide variety of medical issues for the community. Some rumors had it that we would have as many as five nurses at a time, along with a mental health specialist and an occasional visiting doctor. For the most part, the medical staff was separately managed. Although we did communicate with them often, they had their own separate structure and chain of command.

It is typical in a Red Cross shelter to have separate sleeping areas for the staff. I had two choices for where I could set up my cot with pad. The first was a kindergarten classroom that had been designated for staff. It was marginally air conditioned and already had about 12 cots in it. My second choice was the gymnasium, which was primarily being used as the supply room with great quantities of boxed cots, food, bottled water, and other supplies. The air conditioning in it was working fairly well, and there was clearly a lot more room to spread out and privacy created by the boxes stacked five foot high or more. I chose that option. I staked out my area by putting a cot and my gear along the wall in a far corner, hopefully far away from any snoring comrades. I noted the irony of the initial instructions to bring three days' supply of food and water, given that my cot was within 50 feet of several hundred cases of bottled water and several years' worth of food. (Of course, I understood that the Red Cross would have had no way to predict the circumstances of any one particular deployment, and they were just being safe.)

My sleeping location in the gym at Gulfport Central Elementary School

Having never been given an official Red Cross nametag or card, I simply wrote my name on the upper right portion of my Red Cross vest with a Sharpie marker. This piece of clothing was handy in that it had many generously-sized pockets. I soon established a habit of carrying a steno pad, a smaller notepad, a pen or two, a Sharpie marker, a cell phone, sometimes a camera and, of course, a bottle of Purell sanitizer. The small notepad was used for writing people's names and cell phone numbers, along with reminders for tasks that needed to be done. The larger steno pad was an aid to writing a personal journal, with my initial plan being to keep it up on a daily basis. At the end of this day, and without having used the steno pad, I realized that this job was going to be too full and intense to be able to remember it all at the end of each day without taking notes throughout the day. So I began using the steno pad for that purpose. The next night, I would come to the conclusion that there was absolutely no way I would have the energy and time to keep up with writing a journal while in Gulfport, so I decided to do as good of a job as possible in keeping notes as reminders of events, thoughts and feelings, and that I would write the journal after returning home.

I am used to getting in some bona fide exercise at least four times a week, whether bicycling, running, cardio machines, or weight-bearing exercises. I knew and accepted the fact that I would be limited in what I could do during these two weeks, but I was hoping to at least get in an occasional run. I was obviously deriving some exercise benefit from my work, as I was on my feet with a lot of walking around the shelter for much of my long work days. However, I still wanted to get away from the shelter, if only briefly, to have a break from the constant barrage of questions and issues to deal with and to see some of the surrounding area.

So, I was able to steal away for a 40-minute run that evening, knowing that I would have to be back before the city's 8:00 pm curfew. My run gave me the chance to gain my bearings around the neighborhood. Gulfport is definitely not a city set up for pedestrians or joggers, as few sidewalks were evident to me. I had to be careful while running, not only because I had to run alongside the roads without sidewalks, but also because I had to avoid all sorts of hurricane debris, trash, and occasional downed power lines. As I was running, there was a noticeable stench for much of the distance. One conspicuous component of it was the road-kill smell of organic rot and death, which I knew from thousands of miles of bicycle touring. Many trash and debris piles draped the sides of the roads in both residential and commercial areas and also in a less-developed area with a creek/bayou, from which the odor likely emanated. I found myself speculating about the type of remains that were the source of the smells. Probably wild animals such as raccoons or deer, but maybe some pets too. I couldn't avoid thinking of the grim possibility that there could still be human bodies in some of those piles, given the extensive dimensions of the disaster area and the limited resources to search it all.

When I returned, I noticed an additional Gulfport police vehicle in the school parking lot. They were making a shift change, which they did about every 12 hours. It was a mixed feeling knowing that we had 24-hour police staffing (with one officer)—a bit of a secure feeling knowing they were on site, but a little disconcerting about the need for them in the first place. As I later learned, they didn't provide as much true security as one might think. They were doing their best, but you had to keep in mind that they were extremely tired and stressed. Most of the time the officer would be just sitting in the police car or in the small room in the school set up as an office, with the door closed. The officer would be watching television or reading. At least there was a policeman close by if we needed him (and we did on several occasions to come).

Before going to sleep at about 11:30 p.m., as I was going through my luggage I discovered touching and supportive notes and photos from my wife Lisa and my son Austin. I read them with great fondness. As I dozed off to sleep, I heard the loud snoring of Tim, another Red Cross volunteer, off in another corner of the gym. I was so tired it did not bother me in the least.

# 3

## *Jumping in With Both Feet*

o o o o o o o o o o o o o o o o o o o o o o o o o o o o o o o o o o

*Dance like nobody's watching; love like you've never been hurt. Sing like nobody's listening; live like it's heaven on earth.*

—*Mark Twain*

**Monday, September 12**

*Facing a torrent of criticism over the federal response to Hurricane Katrina, Michael Brown resigned today as director of the Federal Emergency Management Agency. David Paulison was named the acting director. The resignation caused little surprise, coming three days after the president relieved him of duties in the hurricane zone and sent him home.*

*President Bush, in his third personal visit to the Gulf Coast since Katrina hit, toured sites in New Orleans and Gulfport, Mississippi.*

I woke up at 6:45 a.m., threw on my shorts, t-shirt, socks, shoes, and Red Cross vest, and in less than five minutes was "at work and on duty." I noticed George in another corner of the gym just starting to rustle around and wake up. Jill was probably still getting some much-needed sleep in the other staff sleeping room, as I'm sure she had been up until very late trying to wrap up lists of information for us and other tasks prior to her leaving tomorrow. With my having been introduced the day before as the new assistant manager, I became the target for any issues or problems needing resolution. It began with June catching sight of me and asking, "Could you give me some help with setting up the breakfast table? We've already got people waiting." I followed her lead in placing breakfast cereals, oranges, snack bars, milk, and plastic utensils on the folding table. Apparently the breakfast setup was usually done by a Red Cross volunteer who had worked late and overslept. June was a wonderful client in her senior years who was volunteering and helping out as much as many of the regular Red Cross volunteers.

Right on the heels of completing that chore was the need to deal with several clients who were upset with inaccurate information regarding the distribution of Red Cross funds, an issue that would remain a persistent problem throughout my two weeks. In the midst of putting out that fire a staff person informed me that we had lost water pressure within the building and that we would need to detour people from the bathroom toilets to the Porta-Toilets outside. Glancing at my watch, I noticed that all of the preceding activity had transpired in a scant 15 minutes.

A bit later, George and I discussed some specifics for making the transition from Jill's outstanding management to our tenure. We felt that she had done an incredible job of moving it from utter anarchy and chaos to a reasonable semblance of order. Our task would be to take it to a higher level of organization, predictability, and maybe comfort. One of the many challenges in managing any Red Cross shelter is that your staff is not only comprised of volunteers, but also that it is always in a state of transition and evolution because the length and timing of commitments vary. For example, September 22nd would be my last full day, while George's tenure was a week longer.

Within the small room designated as the shelter manager's office, George wanted to provide more of a physical buffer from the clients and staff so that he could focus primarily on the desk work associated with his management duties. We decided that Dawn, who had come with us to the shelter, would be a great candidate for an executive secretary, for lack of a better title. She accepted the appointment, and we set her up with a small desk facing the entrance to the room. With this arrangement, Dawn could screen people coming into the office, either handling the problem herself or passing it on to the appropriate person. This change would later turn out to be one of our two best management decisions. With her secretarial and detail-oriented background, Dawn proved to be incredibly dedicated, thorough, and organized. My role was to be more of the hands-on guy to help resolve a wide assortment of issues and problems that cropped up.

In front of us lay many details associated with raising our shelter and its management up to the next level, not the least of which was the acquisition of basic office supplies. That we were not allowed to use the school's office supplies was perfectly understandable. The other volunteer that came with us, Frank, had brought his laptop computer. However, we did not have a printer or a photocopier, and there would certainly be a need for both. I was pretty confident that we would not be able to obtain either from Red Cross, so we decided to just do whatever needed to be done. We talked with some of the clients who knew the area and received second-hand information that there was an office supply store open about four miles away. (At this time, fewer than one quarter of the stores, banks, and gas stations were open for business.) We knew that we could at least purchase a reasonable quality printer for under $100, and it might even have photocopying capability. We only had one Red Cross debit card among us, and it wasn't really meant for purchasing office supplies. I wasn't sure if the purchase would later qualify for reimbursement, but if not, I thought I would just view it as a worthy donation. I handed Frank $100.00 of the $160.00 in cash that I had brought so that he could make the purchase. Jill happened to notice this, looked around quickly, and gave me an anxious, wide-eyed look. She explained that it might be prudent in this environment to be a bit more discreet about whipping out $20 bills within plain view. I duly noted the comment. Over the next few weeks, I observed several other Red Cross volunteers helping out by making sim-ilar donated purchases of needed supplies.

Over the course of my two weeks, I had occasion to meet and become fairly well-acquainted with perhaps 40 hurricane victims as I took care of situations and issues that were presented to me or that I took on as part of my loosely-defined job description. Often, I did so as a function of my initiative and desire to help and meet people, separate from my specific Red Cross role. Most of the time, it all merged together anyway.

Of those 40 or so people, there are about a dozen of which I will always have a vivid recollection. The first of them was Clare, whom I met on this first full day at the shelter. She was not staying at our shelter but lived in the neighborhood, and she would come by occasionally for meals and to use our cell phones. As with most of the people that I spoke with, Clare had lost nearly all of her belongings to the hurricane. She was struggling with cleaning her rental apartment and ridding it of the health-endangering mold. She wasn't sure if it would be condemned or not. Maybe in her late 40's or early 50's, white and slim, Clare had a gentle and caring spirit about her.

Clare shared many things about herself. At the age of 19 she lost most of her memory in a car accident in front of a monastery. Within another two years, while she was rebuilding her memory, both of her parents died. In recent years, she had wanted to make a religious commitment by joining that same monastery or another one nearby, but she said that she had been denied for reason of age. In our conversation, Clare expressed her struggle with interpreting God's messages, especially as related to the hurricane. "What does God want me to learn out of this?" she wondered. "Is it to teach me to not be too attached to my possessions and to focus more on Him?" I certainly didn't have those answers, but I did sympathize with the challenge of discerning divine messages. Clare was interested to hear that I was working on finding direction and purpose in my life by listening to my heart and spirit more, with less of a cognitive approach. We talked briefly about the interplay of providence, in which God's plan is manifested, and free will, whereby we express our God-given ability to choose and direct our own lives.

When I volunteered with the Red Cross, I hoped to be placed in a situation that enabled me to provide direct assistance to people in need, both in my Red Cross role and outside of it. For example, I knew that many people in Fort Collins were ready and willing to help out with relocating receptive hurricane victims through free lodging, employment, and other services. I was determined to constantly keep my radar up for people who might want to be assisted in that way. Although I did not consciously develop a specific list of criteria for a likely candidate, I did have a loosely-formulated image of such a person. To begin with, he or she would need to express something that would indicate a desire to start over, or possibly relate frustrations with the current situation, which relocating might help resolve. Secondly, such a person would need to exhibit the character traits of courage, strength, and hope as opposed to bitterness and a sense of entitlement. I would need to have the sense that this person would be truly appreciative of receiving a community's generosity and would make the most of the opportunity.

Clare was the first person who seemed to fit these criteria. "Clare," I began, "there's a Benedictine monastery near Fort Collins, Colorado, where I live. Maybe they don't have the same age criteria for being accepted. I have no idea if you'd be interested in moving but if you did, I could sure help you with the process." By her reaction, however, I sensed that Clare was well-rooted to the Gulfport area. She did say that she would give it some thought.

Another memorable person that I met on this day was a client named Lamar, a soft-spoken and somber older black gentleman who having suffered a stroke needed a walker to get around. He owned a very old, beat-up, faded-red pickup truck which had a large hole in the floorboard and a vice-grips tool permanently clamped in place for rolling up and down the window. Each day, Lamar would slowly shuffle out to his truck in the parking lot, load up his walker in the back bed, laboriously lift himself into the driver's seat, and go for a drive. I got the impression he just wanted to get away from the shelter for a while, a desire that was perfectly understandable. On this day, I assisted him in his journey out to his truck. While we were slowly walking, Lamar said, "I could use a shoelace." Glancing at his lace-less left shoe, I replied, "There might be one with all of those donated clothes. I'll take a look for you while you're out." Before he returned, I was able to scrounge through a huge pile of unsorted, donated used clothes that was lining one of our hallways and find a black shoelace for him. That simple act brought a big smile to Lamar's face.

Visiting with Clare and Lamar reminded me of one particular side-effect of living through a disaster. Many people want to share their story, which I think helps to process the experience and derive meaning from it. I recalled that I had been more extroverted and self-disclosing than usual after my family and I suffered losses in the Spring Creek flood. In this condition, people become more reflective and open to sharing with strangers than they might with a friend or family member. Perhaps it's the perception of anonymity since the stranger will likely never be seen again. I served in that receptive stranger role many times in Gulfport. At first I was hesitant to ask open-ended, seemingly invasive questions about people's lives and experiences, especially knowing how emotional it might be for them. Gradually, though, I gained more comfort in such an exchange, as it became apparent that most folks were perfectly fine with it and appreciated being asked.

Throughout this Monday, we were visited by five or six groups representing various federal, state, and non-profit agencies, including different factions of the FEMA, National Guard, and medical staff volunteering from other states. These visits proved to be a continual occurrence and I could not keep track of them all. Typically they were assessing what needs we had, if any, relative to what they could provide. In virtually all cases they could not provide a service or supplies that we needed, or what they could offer we already had covered. They were always well-intentioned people, and from one perspective it was an indicator that there was adequate staffing if they were checking in with us. Furthermore, I can fully appreciate the enormity of this catastrophe and the difficulty in organizing an agency's efforts to deal with it. Nonetheless, there was a disturbing degree of redundancy, inefficiency, and lack of communication through it all, both between these groups and within the groups individually. If I was witnessing this disorganization from the perspective of one shelter, it certainly seemed plausible that it was also occurring throughout the overall relief effort.

During the evening, I took a few minutes to catch up on the news. We would usually have a few issues of the local newspaper, the Gulfport *SunHerald*, lying around the front area of the school. Every day or two, I would spend about ten minutes to glance at the local news, as another means of learning about the area and the hurricane's effects. In this day's newspaper, I read an article stating that many of the people of the Mississippi coast were feeling left out of the recovery effort in comparison to all of the media attention and money being funneled into New Orleans. Later, I heard this sentiment expressed by several local residents. They comprehended the reason, given the stature of New Orleans and the sensational nature and drama of what happened there, but that understanding didn't lessen the feeling of being disregarded.

Falling to sleep is usually not an issue for me, especially when hitting the sack at 11:30 p.m. after a long and exhausting day. However, for most of the nights during this adventure, sleep evaded me for another 30 minutes or so. Sometimes it was from not being able to disengage my mind from problem-solving, but most of the time it was because of the lingering adrenaline of the day.

## Tuesday, September 13

*The rebuilding of New Orleans—how to finance it, what to do with neighborhoods that will need to be razed, how to make it less susceptible to future hurricane damage, and the degree to which government should control it—is a hot topic of conversation, with a diversity of opinions.*

*Representatives from the Community Foundation of Northern Colorado and the United Way of Larimer County travel to Louisiana to begin distributing $490,000 in local donations and one-to-one matching funds from the Bohemian Foundation.*

At about 6:30 a.m., still in slumber, I heard a faint voice saying "Jim, wake up. There's a line of people outside expecting to receive their checks from the Red Cross." It took a minute to realize that it was not a dream, and I opened my eyes to see Ashley, one of our Red Cross staff. She continued with her explanation. "Some local radio station announced that we're one of the locations set up to distribute the checks today," Ashley informed me. I hurriedly dressed, ran my hand through my hair to serve as combing for the day, and went out front to find out what was going on. About ten people lingered in line, and they told me their version of what they had heard on the broadcast. We had heard nothing of the sort from Red Cross, and we were clearly not prepared to hand out money. As far as I knew, our services were limited to shelter, food, and medical assistance. Nevertheless, I knew from my short time on board that things could change at any minute and that accurate information and effective communication should not be assumed. I had also learned that the most effective strategy for solving a problem in this environment was to tackle it head-on. Very few problems arose for which it was necessary, appropriate, and/or more efficient for me to consult with a supervisor or to delegate. There was clearly not a rigid chain of command structure, and everyone else, whether above me or below me on the organizational chart, was usually overwhelmed with their own problems to resolve.

So I quickly looked up and called the phone number for the radio station. The disc jockey explained, "We've been doing our best to announce a wide variety of hurricane relief services, with many of those offered by the Red Cross. We try to be clear about what's being offered where, but our listeners sometimes still get confused." This information left me with the unpleasant task of telling these people that they were in the wrong place for receiving the money. I could only tell them what I knew about the process, which was not news to them. They were clearly disappointed and frustrated.

The confusion of how and where to acquire funding from Red Cross became an extremely common occurrence for the duration of my deployment. Initially we were told that people had to call a single toll-free number, become registered, and then proceed to some designated local bank, credit union, or Western Union. We heard from literally dozens of people who had spent multiple hours hitting a redial button (if they were lucky enough to own a cell phone and obtain a good signal through their service carrier) trying to get through to that number, even at 2:00 to 4:00 a.m. I heard of absolutely no one who was able to get through. Everyone would vent their frustration on us. We could only tell them to keep trying, and that each time it was busy it meant that someone else had gotten through, and it verified that the system was working (a positive reframe, if ever there was one). These people were understandably at their wits' end, feeling that they had been given the run-around with FEMA, Red Cross, and other organizations for weeks.

There is no denying that the system of distributing Red Cross funding was hopelessly under-staffed and poorly communicated, at least by typical American standards, once again an indicator that there was no precedent for a disaster of this magnitude. We were a Red Cross shelter, and we received no advance notice from Red Cross about where the funds would be distributed. We learned more from reading the local newspaper and listening to the "word on the street." After several days with the toll-free number clearly not meeting the demand, Red Cross began to set up distribution points around the community where people could go personally to receive their checks. We would hear on one afternoon that the checks had been distributed at a certain community center, for example, but there would be 400 to 500 people in line by 7:00 a.m. and they would then turn people away. People would then go to that location the next day, and the Red Cross might have moved it to another location. By the time one read it in the newspaper, it was probably too late in the day to make the cutoff, and it might or might not be at that same location the next day.

To add another degree of sadness to the issue, these thousands of people were committing all of this effort—hours on end trying to reach someone on a phone line, driving or walking all over town, and standing in line—for the grand total of $360 per person in the family. To many of these people, that money would be the saving grace for being able to buy some gas, pay a few bills, and maybe replace a couple of items lost to the hurricane.

Even getting oneself to a given community location presented another layer of challenge. Many people had lost their vehicles to the hurricane, and the public bus system was exceedingly limited in routes and availability. Even if one did have a vehicle, he or she would be confronted with horrific traffic congestion caused by U.S. 90 no longer open, most traffic lights being down, and more people in town from the influx of aid agency workers and contractors. This problem was yet another example of the extensive impact of the hurricane, all the way down to the simple tasks and conveniences that were normally taken for granted.

At about 9:00 a.m., we had our staff meeting, which George and I had arranged for the purpose of saying goodbye to Jill and to become more organized with our staff. Under Jill's reign, it was in too much of a crisis mode to even think about the luxury of a staff meeting. Most of the staff was able to attend, although we had to have a couple of folks out front to take care of any issues with clients or other people walking in. Some members of the staff had created a going-away bouquet for Jill that consisted of common supplies seen around the shelter, such as toothbrushes, Sharpie markers and, you guessed it, Purell hand sanitizer. It was quite creative, and Jill was touched. George said a few words of appreciation about the incredible job that she had done, we all applauded her, and that moment was effectively the end of Jill's work (other than hurriedly taking care of a few more tasks before rushing off to catch her flight).

Our meeting then quickly transitioned into a muddled attempt by George and me to create some more structure to the staff's duties and their work schedules. George and I had prepared for the meeting by thinking of all of the typical work categories, such as registration, food services, cleaning, and security assistance. Doing so made sense as an exercise for the two of us to get a handle on all of the tasks that needed to be accomplished, but we naively thought that we could have our staff members volunteer for these various categories. Big mistake.

Most of the staff had already been at the shelter for multiple days, and they had meshed themselves into a work routine that seemed to accomplish all of the necessary tasks. Although some people had clear preferences for certain duties, most of the volunteers just viewed themselves as general shelter workers, willing and able to do whatever needed to be done. It was pointed out to us that there was way too much overlap between the various work tasks to think of them as being discrete. No one wanted to be pigeon-holed into only being able to do one type of work, whatever it was. So we made the second of our two best management decisions—to be flexible enough to learn from what the staff was telling us, which clearly was accurate.

After the meeting, I continued my organizational tasks by setting up a schedule for the staff's off days, in a way that was as agreeable as possible to all. According to George, the Red Cross standard was to receive one day off if a person had made a two-week commitment and two days off if he or she had made a three-week commitment.

My final organizing task of the day was to set everyone up on a loosely-defined work schedule so that we could depend on a person being on duty at a certain time. The expectation was for being 12 hours on and 12 hours off. I was able to obtain everyone's commitment to a certain 12-hour period that covered all of the busiest times of the day, in addition to having at least two people awake through the night.

George and I decided that we should offset our work periods, so that at least one of us was awake and on-duty between 7:00 a.m. and 11:00 p.m. I offered to take 11:00 a.m. to 11:00 p.m., if he was all right with 7:00 a.m. to 7:00 p.m. He agreed. That schedule turned out to be utterly pointless. Not once were we able to keep to that guideline. There was always more work to be done than staff members available, and if you were in the building you were subject to being presented with a problem to resolve. It basically became a 6:30 a.m. to 11:30 p.m. or later job, with a few self-enforced breaks thrown in. For my part, I took mini-breaks to make phone calls home, eat some of my food in the sanctity of my cot area (I wasn't about to carry any of that food back home), and on a few occasions go for a run.

That evening, a deaf man came into the shelter, anxiously looking for his brother. He scribbled his name and that of his brother on a note. The typical Red Cross procedure is to keep the names of all clients confidential, meaning that anyone coming to the front desk and asking for a client is told, "We will look for him, and if he's here, we'll tell him that you would like to see him. However, it is his choice whether or not to see you, and we can't confirm if he is or isn't here, without his permission." This procedure presented a real dilemma in cases where very distraught people came in or called to find out if a missing relative or friend happened to be in the shelter. I could only imagine the anxiety of not knowing if one's friend or family member was alive or dead while trying desperately to locate him or her. I wasn't about to respond to such a request with, "I can't tell you if that person is here or not." In my mind, the only justified situation for using that response would be if that client *was* in our shelter and he or she had specifically told me not to tell that person. I felt that this was an appropriate case for throwing out the rule book and using good judgment. At any rate, this man was already walking down the hallway, so I wasn't going to order him back out. About the time that I recognized his brother's name as a person who had previously registered, he saw his brother down the hall and ran to warmly embrace him. The intensity of their emotions led me to suspect that they had been separated during the hurricane and hadn't known the fate of each other.

Soon thereafter, Maddy and Shelly, two staff members, reported that while they were on the north side of the building washing out some dishes, they were approached by Leroy, one of our clients recognized as an active drug user. He was apparently asking them some questions about how much money they had, which made them nervous. I advised them to make sure that there was another volunteer—preferably a male—whenever they were in an isolated area like that. Additionally, I mentioned it to the police officer and he said that he would watch him more closely.

In the late evening, George felt faint and was examined by the nurses. It had been a very hot and strenuous day. The nurses recommended that to keep himself a bit cooler he not wear his hat. George explained that he liked to wear the hat because it made it easier for people to identify him as the manager in a crowd or down a hallway (as in, "Go talk to that fellow over there with the hat.") "That could be," the nurse responded, "but I think you'd be much more effective managing the shelter without a hat, as opposed to keeping the hat on and ending up in a hospital bed." He concurred.

At a little after 11:00 p.m., some police officers arrived and told us that they were aware of about 20 people who needed shelter. They wondered if we had room for them. With flashlights in hand, we did a quick assessment of our hallways and the stage area in the auditorium. We decided that we could probably squeeze them in. However, we then found out from the officers that they were not hurricane victims, but rather contractors from some other part of the country looking for work and needing shelter. George decided that it would not be appropriate for us to give up space for them, so we rejected the request.

With that decision made at 11:20 p.m., I went to my cot to crash. I was in bed for about ten minutes and very close to sleep, when I heard Jeremy's voice telling me, "There are 20 Mexican workers at our front door and they want a place to sleep." With that bit of news, I stumbled out of the cot, haphazardly dressed, and went out front. Through Donna, one of our staff who was bilingual, we found out that they were just looking for a place to shower and to sleep until about 4:30 a.m., at which time they would be leaving for work. It was surprising that they were able to travel to the shelter without being apprehended, given the 8:00 p.m. curfew in the city. We took pity on them, although we did not want to wake up everyone in the hallway with their taking showers one by one in the lone shower. So we told them that they could use the hose outside, and we carefully advised them—through Donna—to make sure they didn't get the non-potable water in their eyes or mouths. With that completed, I went back to my cot at 11:45 p.m., exhausted and ready for six or seven hours of good sleep.

So I thought. Not quite asleep, I began to hear singing and guitar-playing from the front of the school. While the city of Gulfport had a curfew of 8:00 p.m. and we had a supposed curfew of 11:00 p.m. for our clients to be inside the building, there was an enforcement laxity, especially for clients wanting to smoke cigarettes in the middle of the night. This situation was taking it too far, though, as Jeremy and Trevor, our twenty-something, sociable staffers, were apparently leading a Kumbaya session of blues and rock classics. Although it would have been appreciated at a normal hour of the day or evening, it wasn't at this time. I was too tired to rise from bed to shut it down, so I ended up speaking with them about it the next day. My dreams had musical accompaniment until about 2:00 a.m.

## Wednesday, September 14

*Officials estimate that 75 percent of the 1,000 Hurricane Katrina evacuees in Denver will decide to make Colorado their new home, rather than return. About 100 have already found jobs. The evacuees are being assisted in located employment, housing, and financial aid.*

*State and federal officials report that they are scouring the Southeast for up to 300,000 recreation vehicle travel trailers and mobile homes that can be offered as free or subsidized housing for as long as two years, the time it could take some people to rebuild or find new permanent homes in the affected areas of Mississippi, Alabama, and Louisiana. Finding suitable locations to place the trailers and mobile homes is proving a challenge.*

Tim served as my alarm clock around 7:00 a.m. when he noisily loaded up bags of ice to take up front. Each day we received about 30 ten-pound bags that we used in five large coolers filled with bottled water and other drinks. I rolled out of my cot, put on my "uniform" of shorts, t-shirt, Red Cross vest, athletic socks and shoes, stretched my arms, rubbed my eyes, and went out to the hallway to begin the day.

The first memorable person I met on this Wednesday was Trent. He wasn't staying at the shelter, but he stopped by every day or two to visit or use a cell phone. Upon first seeing him, one might guess that he was a professional athlete and/or an actor. About 6' 4", he looked about 30 years old. Possessing a very athletic build and strikingly handsome features, Trent also was well-dressed whenever he came by. Correspondingly, there was about him an extraordinary self-confidence and presence that distinguished him in our crowd of folks. I engaged him in conversation, finding him to be friendly and articulate. Trent was living in Gulfport and had suffered some damage to his home. I wasn't sure of all of the details, but I gathered that he was in between jobs when the hurricane hit. He was looking for a professional position, but was willing to do whatever was necessary to earn money. Trent's recent employment had been in various academic management positions at Florida International University, where he was expecting to complete a Masters of Education and a B.S. in Political Science within two years. A fallback option being considered was enlisting in the U.S. Navy for submarine duty. Looking up at his tall frame, I asked him the obvious question, "Aren't you too tall to qualify for submarine duty?" "I'm just barely under the maximum," Trent answered. As part of his job search, several days later he gave me a copy of his resume. On his resume, I noticed that he had been awarded a Division I basketball scholarship to FIU in 1991 through 1993 and that he had a graduate school GPA of 3.9. This was clearly a person who would be going somewhere with his life. This encounter made me think that it would be very enjoyable and meaningful to be able to follow the path of these many people I was meeting, both volunteers and clients. Unfortunately though, I knew that in the vast majority of cases that would not happen.

We would occasionally see a few of the school staff—including the principal—at the school attending to their office work. For the most part, they stayed in the office area, which was locked and unavailable to us, although they would infrequently stroll through the hallways. I got the impression that they had mixed feelings about all of this happening to their school, even though the clients were residents of their own community. Despite Red Cross's policy of doing whatever was necessary to return a building to its original condition, I certainly couldn't blame them for not wanting their classrooms and offices used, given the lack of respect that many of our clients were demonstrating with their littering and unclean habits.

During the morning, we learned that the school was intending to begin classes again on Monday, October 3rd, only two and one-half weeks away. By looking at the current condition of the place and thinking about how much time it would take to clean everything and return it to its original order, the facility's life as a shelter seemed near its end. As a first step in that process, the school wanted us to move everyone out of the back hallway and become consolidated in the front hallways and the auditorium. This ended up taking several days, as a portion of these people had seemingly grown roots with their scattered belongings. We handled it delicately and diplomatically at first, but after little progress by the end of the next day, we were moving their belongings to the other hallway ourselves.

There was no shortage of food at this point in the disaster, now 16 days after the hurricane hit, at least not at our shelter. The gymnasium was stocked with dozens of pallets of non-perishable food, such as canned goods, pasta, cereals, powdered milk, energy bars, and, of course, M.R.E.'s, the legendary Meals Ready to Eat. Although they have been a staple of the military and the Red Cross for many years, it was my first experience with them. Each meal is contained in one foil-lined bag almost the size of a desk-sized dictionary. Inside are smaller foil-lined packages of the various components of the meal, including all spices and plastic utensils needed. With many dozens of different meals to choose from, it would take a much-longer deployment than I would be interested in to sample all of them. People who are connoisseurs of M.R.E.'s have their favorites, as some are clearly better than others. I tried about three different ones. Spaghetti with meat sauce was my favorite. M.R.E.'s are surprisingly tasty in my opinion, but a downside is that they generate an incredible amount of trash. I have never seen so much packaging for one meal! I realize that environmental stewardship is not the primary objective for these meals, but it seems that you'd need a Humvee per three soldiers just to carry the trash. The coolest thing about an M.R.E. is the heating device. It's some chemical (probably top secret) that, with the addition of a small amount of water, generates enough heat to cook the meal. This chemical is in—surprise!—a foil-lined bag, and you place any of the food bags in it to heat them up.

Because the M.R.E.'s were a bit of a luxury and more oriented towards emergency food, we didn't use them to serve our clients. (I later read that the U.S.

government purchases the M.R.E.'s at a unit price of $7.50.) Instead, we had a self-serve breakfast table that featured cold cereal, powdered milk, fresh fruit (if we had it), and juice. For lunch and dinner, we served hot meals that were prepared by the North Carolina Baptist Men's Disaster Relief organization, delivered (or sometimes picked up by us) in an insulated container called a Cambro. These meals were about on par with a typical school lunch—not great, but okay given the circumstances. They were served on tables set up outside underneath the overhang. Clients and staff were directed to eat outside, which lessened the need for inside cleanup. The inside breakfast table also served as a snack table, making food available 24 hours per day. The foods that I most missed were fresh fruit and vegetables.

Since the front overhang area offered the opportunity to smoke and a break from being inside, and since meals were served there, it functioned as the front porch of our shelter. The front steps, relocated children's chairs, old sofa, and curbs provided seating. This area, along with the entry area just inside the school, is where 90 percent of the shelter's newsworthy action took place.

Setting up for dinner in front of
the Gulfport Central Elementary School shelter

Having now worked with the staff for about three long and full days, I was feeling that I had a general impression of each of them. For me, there was a growing sense of camaraderie and attachment to many of the individuals of our team. Normally I wouldn't think that I could become that well-acquainted with a group in such a short time, but given that we were going through such adversity and intense experiences together, it drastically lessened the required time. The ages of our group of 18 ranged from maybe 20 years old to several in their mid-60's. All were white and most were from the eastern third of the country. Every one of us was genuinely committed to making a difference, and it was interesting to observe how we each felt best able to do that. The structure was quite loose as compared with most work settings—or even volunteer settings for that matter—and it demanded that we each be self-motivated, self-directed, and with strong initiative. All of us met those criteria, in my view. While nearly all of the staff would have accepted a particular work assignment with a good attitude, that approach wasn't often needed. Ninety-five percent of the work was accomplished by the staff falling into a groove oriented towards their particular personality and interests and being self-directed in performing the tasks. Amazingly, it just seemed to all work out right, analogous to not assigning food categories for a pot-luck dinner, and ending up with a healthy and balanced meal.

Some of the staff members were more clearly the social ones, with one young woman connecting so well with the younger male clients that it would strike most people as flirtatious. Other people gravitated toward taking care of the food-related duties. Carl was the designated driver since he had arrived with a Red Cross issued sport utility vehicle. With some assistance from others, he also did the majority of the mopping, trash removal, and cleanup. Frank was our information technology expert because he had arrived with his laptop computer and was obviously skilled in that area. He also helped Tim with the registration duties and occasionally subbed for Dale, Jeremy, Trevor, or Sam on the graveyard shift. George took care of most of the communication with upper management in the Red Cross and did most of the managerial desk work. I assisted him with various managerial duties and also tried to resolve whatever seemed to be the biggest problem or the most pressing need at any particular time. These duties ran the gamut from cleaning the bathroom floor to dealing with a suicide threat. Flexibility, pacing myself, and creative problem-solving were essential. Dawn efficiently took care of all sorts of administrative work, with much of it on cell phones or the computer.

As would be expected with a diverse group of 18 strangers thrown together under adverse circumstances, bickering, petty grievances, and drama occasionally occurred. For the most part though, the operation went rather smoothly. If one staff member had a personality conflict with or dislike for another staff member, he or she seemed to recognize it and simply avoid that person. The diversity of work and flexibility of the system allowed them to do so. Several cliques germinated within the staff, and they tended to work together and take their day off together.

Compared to our group of shelter workers, it did seem that the nurses had more issues of conflicting personalities and squabbling. From an outsider's perspective, I would chalk that up to two things that distinguished them from us. First, they were all performing duties related to their profession. More technical skill was involved, and this fact could lead to differences of opinion about procedures. In short, there was inherently more ego involved. Secondly, the medical staff, sometimes numbering five or six people, was crammed into an office measuring no more than 10 feet by 10 feet. They did also set up a table outside for administering shots—which allowed a few of them separate space—but they were clearly more confined than our shelter workers were.

With all the emotional and physical intensity, humor was a great stress reliever. Good-natured pranks made us occasionally feel like being at a summer camp. Several of the women picked on Jeremy, Trevor, and Sam, the three youngest men. Sam seemed to receive the brunt, including a large pile of boxed feminine hygiene products on his cot. Another time during the midday, he was asleep to the point of near unconsciousness, due to being on duty throughout the previous night. Robyn and Valerie couldn't pass the opportunity up; they wrote "left arm" on his left arm and "right arm" on his right arm, an apparent editorial comment on his intelligence. He was actually a sharp fellow but just had a personality that was subject to teasing. On another occasion, Robyn decided to have a little spontaneous fun by demonstrating the pyrotechnic skills that she had presumably picked up while in the army. Outside of the building and away from the view of any of the clients, five of us watched the performance. One notable feature of this explosive display was that the only materials needed are commonly available in a Red Cross shelter: the heating chemical from an M.R.E. and a 16-ounce plastic water bottle. Robyn's instructions were very straightforward. Simply place the chemical in the plastic bottle, add a little water, screw the cap on, and run. As any good physics student could predict, the rapidly heated water expands the air in the bottle, which swells the bottle to the point that it looks like a bloated, transparent sausage. Then, kablam! We were all very entertained and impressed! Recalling my adolescence, I would say that the decibels were about midway between a cherry bomb and an M-80. (Of course, in no way am I suggesting that you try this at home—or any other location!)

Speaking of supplies, on more than a few instances I found myself recalling rerun episodes of the television show, MASH. Yes, everyone was doing the best that they could, but after three consecutive days of ordering and re-ordering specific supplies, only to have a truck deliver items that we didn't even need, the situation became frustratingly comical. In the most extreme case, George included "two folding chairs" on his supplies order list nearly every morning for at least two weeks, and they never arrived. He was never directly promised them by the person receiving his order on the phone, but it seemed like a reasonable request. Fortunately, we weren't in urgent need for any of the items ordered.

Over the course of my two weeks, I witnessed many instances of inefficiency and poor communication with the hurricane relief effort, both within particular agencies and between them. This perception included the Red Cross, but I found myself being much more tolerant of that agency as compared to FEMA and the military. From my perspective, there is an important distinction between tax-supported agencies with paid employees and a non-profit agency operated largely with volunteers. Yes, the inefficiencies and poor communication were frustrating, and certain aspects of the Red Cross operations could have gone better. However, it would be too easy—along with unfair and inaccurate—to jump to conclusions without having a better understanding of the overall picture, which I knew that I did not have. What I did know was that the scale of this disaster was three to four times anything previously experienced in the United States, and even if you could argue that it was predicted and was just a matter of time, it is probably unrealistic to think that a non-profit agency could be geared up to respond to the same standard of quality and efficiency that they meet with a "normal" disaster. Also, I knew that in the case of a major disaster, the entire Red Cross relief model is predicated upon the local chapters forming the foundation of response, with supplemental support then coming from other states and the national headquarters. When the nature of the disaster is so catastrophic that the buildings of the local Red Cross chapters are destroyed, and the administrators and volunteers with those chapters lose their homes and have to evacuate themselves, it creates an additional major hurdle right from the start, which weakens the entire relief process.

Also, I rationalized that the inefficiency that I observed with the Red Cross didn't seem to translate into wasted dollars. The Red Cross's inefficiencies that I experienced centered on ineffective and disorganized processes, particularly communication. But when the work is accomplished by volunteers working at least

12-hour days, that type of inefficiency doesn't really translate into financial waste. Although my perspective was limited in scope, I had no reason to *not* view the Red Cross as an extremely vital organization that manages its considerable financial resources in an appropriate manner.

Out of curiosity, after returning home I researched the effectiveness and financial efficiency of the American Red Cross. I was impressed with what I found. Charity Navigator is a well-established and recognized non-profit group that rates over 5,000 charities for their efficiency and effectiveness with donors' money. It utilizes objective criteria to rate agencies in ten categories related to performance and financial health, with the score then being reported categorically with a four-star rating system. Charity Navigator determined that 91 percent of a donor's dollar to the Red Cross goes towards their programs (the services that they provide) and only 9% goes towards administrative and fundraising costs. They received a rating of four stars, the highest category.[1]

I met a second unforgettable person on this day, despite the fact that I only spent 20 minutes with her at most. A middle-aged white woman, Mary had come to our shelter to obtain some basic cleaning supplies and a tetanus shot. When I first saw her, she was weeping in the entrance area, so I walked with her to a quieter area of the auditorium where we could talk. She proceeded to tell me that she was a high school teacher, living in a subdivision several miles away. "I've lost everything," Mary said, wiping away tears, "including three generations of our family heirlooms. The only clothes that I have left I'm wearing." At some point soon after the hurricane, she had cut herself on a sharp object and the wound had become infected. "A doctor prescribed an antibiotic for me and said that it was essential that I take it, but there weren't any pharmacies open. I went door to door in my neighborhood and finally found someone who happened to have some leftover antibiotic. Fortunately, after a few days of taking the medicine the infection went away."

She was different from most of the hurricane victims with whom I had thus far talked with because she was clearly more well-to-do. She portrayed her neighborhood as being middle to upper income and home to teachers, doctors, lawyers, and other professionals. When she described the location of her neighborhood, at first it did not make sense that they would have suffered that much damage because it was about three miles inland from the railroad tracks. The railroad tracks are parallel to the beach and about one-half mile inland. The vast majority of the devastating damage along the Mississippi coast occurred in the zone between the tracks and the beach. I later looked at a map and saw that within her neighborhood was a bayou that drained straight to the ocean. That explained how the storm surge could have pushed into her neighborhood. I asked, somewhat tentatively, why she and her neighbors did not evacuate. "There wasn't a mandatory evacuation in Gulfport," she answered. "Prior to Katrina our 'worst case scenario' point of reference was Hurricane Camille in 1969. Camille was a Category 5, and it only resulted in about a four-foot storm surge in our neighborhood. Katrina must have come in on a different path, because we had a 15- to 20-feet high surge with it."

Mary expressed that she definitely understood prioritizing the recovery on the area along the beach and in the lower income areas. However, many of the people in her neighborhood were also desperate and in need of assistance. While all of these people presumably had homeowner's insurance, most of them were finding out that their policy didn't cover this type of damage. An ongoing battle was waged between homeowners, insurance companies, and the state attorney general's office over the distinctions between damage from hurricane force winds, storm surges caused by the hurricane, and flooding caused by heavy rain. And, even if they were to eventually acquire coverage, it could be months away and they needed many basic supplies immediately.

Once again, I felt myself growing very frustrated with the lack of immediate assistance for people needing support. For the second time, I felt the strong urge to try to help a person beyond my defined role as a Red Cross volunteer. I said to Mary, "There are many people in my hometown who would love to be able to financially assist hurricane victims, especially if they knew the circumstances and had assurances that it was a worthy recipient." She seemed appreciative of my comment and I gave it more thought before continuing. "Do you know of a community or neighborhood group—preferably a non-profit—that could serve in the role of receiving financial donations and then distributing those funds to the people most in need? It would be best if they already had a structure set up to be able to do that in a very accountable and equitable manner." "Well," she replied, "I'm a member of a Methodist church and we have a pastoral board that could serve that purpose." She gave me a contact name and phone number. Telling her I would give it my best effort, we walked out to the gymnasium to find her some cleaning supplies and food. We then proceeded to the nurse's station so that she could receive her tetanus shot. I gave her a hug and wished her well. As the nurses greeted her, I noticed her eyes tearing up again.

After Mary left, I thought awhile about the hurricane's impact relative to demographics and social class. Although there did seem to be a disproportionate impact on lower income and struggling people along the Mississippi coast and in

New Orleans, it certainly did not spare the more affluent people who happened to be in Katrina's path.

During this same afternoon, I became acquainted with Vinh, a Vietnamese man, maybe 35 years old. He walked through the front doors of our shelter with a handwritten note. Because of the note, I first assumed that he did not speak English but soon found that he spoke it rather fluently. The note was just to aid in clarifying his situation. A Red Cross volunteer by the name of Kylie had found him living on the beach under a tarp for shelter. She learned that he had lost his apartment and worldly possessions in nearby Biloxi. Vinh wanted to relocate to Atlanta where his uncle lived, but he had little money. Kylie somehow made the acquaintance of a woman named Ruth who lived in southern Georgia. Completely on her own initiative, Ruth had loaded up a pickup truck and trailer with non-perishable food and other supplies and driven to the Mississippi coast, distributing it wherever it was needed. The note said that I, as the Red Cross recipient of the note, should contact Ruth, now back at her home in Georgia, regarding an effort to assist Vinh in moving to Atlanta. Vinh and I sat down outside on one of the front steps where he proceeded to fill in some of the details.

"After leaving Vietnam 12 years ago, I lived in California with my family. I also lived in Atlanta for awhile, but I've been in Biloxi for about a year now. I moved here so that I could work on shrimp boats. It's good work and I've liked it," Vinh said.

"How was it for you with the hurricane?" I asked.

"I was off work during the week before it hit, and I hadn't really been paying attention to the news. When I did first hear about its approach on Sunday, they said it was going to be bad, but there wasn't a mandatory evacuation. I thought I'd be fine in my apartment," Vinh explained. "My apartment was on the first floor, and I was there by myself when it hit. The wind and rain got so loud…I was very scared. Wow! The water started seeping under my door and I thought about leaving. It was after daybreak but it was so dark from the clouds and rain that it looked like night. Then a big wave broke through a window and the water started gushing in. I felt panic and didn't know what to do. I thought I would drown if I stayed there, so I climbed out a broken window. I didn't even have time to think about taking anything with me, not even my billfold. The water was very cold. The waves and current were too strong to swim against, so I mostly just tried to keep my head above water. Fortunately it was pushing me further inland. Eventually I got to more shallow water where I could wade, and then out of the water so I could run. I ended up more than a mile from my apartment."

With the strong emotion in his voice, I had the impression that this was the first time Vinh had told anyone his story. He continued. "I ended up finding shelter inside a building on higher ground. There was one other person there, who I didn't know. He told be that we could climb a tall tree if the water kept rising. I was glad to be inside, and didn't want to have to go back outside. The wind was incredible; there were large limbs and even trees being blown down. Wow! Huge pieces of sheet metal from buildings and signs were flying through the air."

Vinh seemed to be reliving his story as he told it, and he needed a minute to calm down. I offered him bottled water and an energy bar that were on a nearby table and he accepted them. "What was it like when you went back?" I asked. "I could not believe what I saw when I returned," he replied. "My apartment building was barely standing. All of my furniture and belongings were completely gone. I have no idea where they went. It was very bad when I learned a neighbor had drowned. Then the worst thing. There was a woman's body stuck in the middle of a tree in our front yard. It looked like she had been swimming for her life, and some of her clothing had gotten tangled up in the tree. They didn't even remove the body for two days! Wow!" Vinh finished his story by mentioning that he had been interviewed by Cable News Network the previous week. Because of his traumatic experience, Vinh desperately wanted to move to Atlanta and to never live near the ocean again. I told him that I would call Ruth and try to help him. He registered at our front desk and carried his small backpack with everything he owned down to the cot set up for him in the auditorium.

A cliché could not be truer than the one, "A crisis brings out the best of people and the worst of people." By this time in my deployment, I felt as if I had observed and listened to enough of the hurricane victims to have a grasp of the range of ways in which they were dealing with their trauma. Of course, dealing with such a tragedy on an emotional, psychological, and spiritual level can be a long process, with a progression of stages. What I witnessed, now 16 days after the hurricane hit, was a broad continuum. Pre-hurricane, many of these people were already quite familiar with challenges and suffering, whether through poverty, homelessness, mental health problems, physical illnesses, injuries, or drug and alcohol addictions. If life had taught them anything, it was how to survive. Although I did not know any of these people prior to the hurricane, I did gain the sense that for a handful of them this was a blow that pushed them over the edge from which they might or might not emotionally recover. A good percentage of the people in our shelter, maybe one-third to one-half, typically exhibited griping, frustration, irritability, or anger in their behavior. But who could blame them for that, given what they had been through? To many of them, the hurricane was just another piece of bad luck to have to deal with. Nothing more, nothing less.

Given this experience, it was all the more remarkable that at least one third of the people I met demonstrated an incredible degree of courage, hope, and compassion. These were the folks who were truly making the best of a bad situation: strengthening their character, gaining spiritual insight, reaching out to help others, establishing meaningful connections, and deriving personal growth. Through my reaching out to help and their sharing themselves at their most vulnerable points, a spiritual connection was established. I felt as if it were another wave of the same divine force that compelled me—and led me—to Gulfport.

At the time I arrived, the shelter had a huge surplus of used clothing. I had observed that quite a few shopping center parking lots had been set up as distribution points for vast quantities of used clothing. In our shelter's case, clothing was no longer needed, so we would have to deal with removing the remainder from the school as part of shutting down the shelter. At the Red Cross headquarters in Gulfport, an enormous pile of donated clothing, several feet high and covering several thousand square feet, was spread out on the ground and available to anyone to pick through. On this Wednesday, more than two weeks after Katrina, few people were taking advantage of it, but the donated clothing continued to arrive. Somewhat humorously, there was a not small accumulation of heavy wool sweaters, winter coats, mittens, and stocking caps, presumably donated by northerners who were uninformed of the lack of need for such clothing in the mild winters of the Gulf Coast. I hoped that this used clothing surplus, which was probably typical of the Louisiana and Mississippi coasts at that time after the hurricane, would not be wasted and would end up with people that needed it. The logistical issues of acquiring the right amount of resources—whether people, water, food, clothing, construction equipment, or whatever—at the right time and in the right place is obviously essential for effective disaster relief, but it is deceptively difficult to achieve.

In the early evening, a heavy-set woman had broken her cot and was basically stranded, because she couldn't rise from it by herself. It took Allen, a male nurse, and me to lift her up. She seemed embarrassed by the situation, and Allen and I did all that we could to dispel that feeling. We told her that we would figure out a more secure system for a cot, and we went to the gym to see what we had for materials. No stronger cots were available, so we had to figure out some way to create additional support for an unbroken replacement of the same cot. We decided to fashion two support columns under each side, but we couldn't find anything that was just the right height. After much trial and error, we ended up building the two columns by duct-taping a tuna fish can to a box of M.R.E.'s. Allen and I had a good laugh when we calculated the total number of years of college that we had between us and the amount of time that it took to figure out a solution to that problem.

Over the course of these first days, I had noticed that a good portion of supplies were identified as having been sent by other countries, including Canada, Mexico, Great Britain, and Japan. When our clients and other local citizens became aware of the extent of the national and international assistance to them, many were astonished and appreciative. They had been so focused on dealing with their problems that they didn't have a sense of the degree to which the Hurricane Katrina news had been carried worldwide.

Even though the number of our clients was not large—usually between 90 and 100—there was a disproportionate degree of medical, criminal, and behavioral problems, due to the nature of our demographics. This day seemed to have even more cases than the norm. A woman was brought in by police, having been recently robbed of her Red Cross money and beaten. She had a very nasty bruised face and black eye. She was tended to by the medical staff, a mental health worker, and then registered to spend the night. Several of us noticed that one of our clients, a diabetic woman about 60 years old, had been sleeping all day and looked extremely pale. The nurses took a closer look at her and ended up having her transported to the hospital. A man by the name of Rocky was accused of fondling one of the women who were contracted by Red Cross to come in each day to help clean the bathrooms. The police did a background check on him and it came back clean. He was added to our growing list of clients to keep a close eye on. I don't recall why we weren't able to throw him out, as we later did with similar cases.

While eating my dinner outside, I noticed that Bill, one of our clients with serious mental health issues, started crying and saying that nobody liked him. Although several other clients looked at him disapprovingly, a Red Cross staff member and an empathetic client tried to comfort him. The next day I observed Bill handing a $20.00 bill to a female client, telling her that God had told him to give it to her. I complimented him on his kindness and he angrily responded that it wasn't his kindness, it was God's. Then I visited for a while with an older white man by the name of Ron who had recently registered as a new client. He had been working on his recently-purchased old pickup truck and was absolutely filthy with grass, grease, and dirt. Through our conversation, I learned that he hated all cops, gays, and most of his family members. It was sad to hear so much anger in one life.

Much to my joy, two of our clients, Dan and Teresa, were taking it upon themselves to help with sweeping and cleaning up cigarette butts in the parking lot. Unfortunately, they were the exception. Even though I could certainly understand the difficult times that our clients were going through and could forgive them for not pitching in to help clean up other people's messes, many of them didn't even bother to clean up their own trash or would throw cigarette butts out in the school parking lot, even with butt containers around.

After complimenting Dan and Teresa on their work, a young Hispanic man named Hector informed me that he wanted to return to Houston, where he lived. He had traveled to Gulfport a few weeks before with his brother, and they had donated their time helping with the recovery. Hector had little money, so I helped him with determining the Greyhound bus schedule out of Biloxi, because the Gulfport station was destroyed. It also took some effort to find public transportation to get him from Gulfport to Biloxi.

I decided that I had met my quotient for adventure and stimulation for one day and fell onto my cot about 11:30 p.m. Before falling asleep, I reflected on my great appreciation for having this opportunity to directly help people, both through my role with the Red Cross and through my own initiative "on the side." I resolved to continue to make the most of my circumstances and to creatively and ardently make things happen.

# 4

# *Shelter Transition*

○ ○ ○ ○ ○ ○ ○ ○ ○ ○ ○ ○ ○ ○ ○ ○ ○ ○ ○ ○ ○ ○ ○ ○ ○ ○ ○ ○ ○ ○ ○ ○ ○ ○

*Opposition is a natural part of life. Just as we develop our physical muscles through overcoming opposition—such as lifting weights—we develop our character muscles by overcoming challenges and adversity.*

*—Stephen Covey, author*

### Thursday, September 15

*Hurricanes as powerful as Katrina have become nearly twice as common in the last 35 years as ocean surface temperatures around the world have warmed, according to a team of climatologists from Georgia and Colorado. "The trend toward more powerful hurricanes is consistent with the theory that human-caused climate change is affecting the violent storms," said Peter Webster, a Georgia Institute of Technology climatologist and lead author of the new report.*

*According to initial Red Cross estimates, more than one-third of the estimated 171,000 dwellings in Mississippi's six coastal counties have been destroyed. Less than ten percent of homes in South Mississippi avoided getting damaged in some way.*

With an early start to the day around 6:30 a.m., I learned from George that he had just found out from the next level up in the Red Cross that our shelter would be closing this coming Saturday, in two days. Although we knew that it was imminent, given that the school was intending to open on October 3rd, we didn't anticipate it being this soon. No associated information was provided regarding relocation of clients or staff. Whether caused by the Red Cross, the school system, the local E.O.C. (Emergency Operations Center), and/or some other agency, this last minute decision-making and inadequate communication had become a distressing pattern.

George immediately went to the front of the school to write on the standing flip, "This shelter is closing on <u>Saturday</u>. Please start packing your belongings." The flip chart was our primary communication method to our clients regarding major news. Several staff members took on the task of hustling boxes from nearby stores, to be used for the packing. This sudden announcement resulted in a perceptible anxiety on the part of the clients, not knowing their fate. One woman complained loudly about the school starting back up so soon. She didn't think it was realistic, given that many of the kids had lost all of their books and supplies and that many of the teachers and students were still evacuated or had moved away indefinitely.

I was lifted from the stress and sobering reality by a black woman's greeting to me to "Have a blessed day." Another phrase that I heard later this day, which I really liked, was from an attractive, thin Asian-Indian woman. When I asked her how she was doing she responded, "I'm blessed."

Fairly early in the morning, a woman by the name of Billie came in the shelter with her handicapped brother and two children. She related that she was from New Orleans and that she had three kids, her disabled brother, and both parents to care for. She was temporarily staying at the home of her parents, a few miles away. She had walked to our shelter, not having a car and with little money. She wanted to know how to obtain the financial assistance from Red Cross, and I had to tell her that it would take more time and patience. Billie also was wondering where she could acquire food stamps and support through the WIC (Women, Infants and Children) program. I asked a client and was told that that service was provided by the Harrison County Department of Human Services at a location that she specified. Through a phone call to the Coast Transit Authority, the local public bus agency, I learned that their shuttle bus route—offering rides at no charge during that time—did include that location. However, neither the client nor the Coast Transit Authority receptionist knew the degree to which the building was affected by the hurricane. I located the Department's phone number in the local phone directory, but not unexpectedly, it was out of service. We decided to take a chance that it was only the phone service that was out, and that the Department of Human Services was still operating out of that building. The shuttle bus arrived at our shelter on schedule within 30 minutes, and I helped get Billie, her brother, and her two children on board, along with some bottled water and snack food.

About an hour and a half later the shuttle bus returned with the same family of passengers. I was disappointed to hear from them and the driver that the county building had been destroyed in the hurricane and that there was no signage about where the food stamps and WIC program were relocated. The woman was understandably dejected. Not knowing what else I could do, I convinced the driver to take them back to her parents' house, so that she didn't have to walk the two miles with her young children and disabled brother in the 90 degree heat. They drove away, leaving me feeling frustrated with the lack of resolution to their problem, and concerned and curious about their eventual fate. Over the course of the two weeks, dozens of similar cases transpired.

Soon thereafter, an Associated Press photographer wandered in, stating to me, "I'm looking for a family to photograph. I'd like to do the shoot this evening, with the family seated in front of a television set watching President Bush address the country about the hurricane relief effort." Over the previous four days, my exposure to national news had been limited to about five minutes of reading a local newspaper, and I was not even aware that President Bush was giving such a talk. "There are a few barriers to that," I told him while he glanced around. "First, we only have two families staying with us. Second, there's no television set here. Lastly, the people staying in our shelter are not very connected to national political news right now. They have more basic needs and issues to deal with at the moment," I said. It would have to be a very contrived photograph, I thought to myself, as I couldn't imagine that they would choose to watch that speech on their own initiative. If there was a television set they would likely choose a program that provided more entertainment and distraction from their struggles. He got the idea and left to continue his search.

For my on-the-side volunteer work, I was able to make some good progress throughout this day. With the previous day's information from Mary, I reached Fred, the pastor at the Methodist church, by cell phone. Fred told me that they had set up a committee to handle the distribution of hurricane relief donations in an equitable and accountable manner. He mentioned that they had already identified 190 church member families without insurance to cover their losses and a highest priority sub-set that was lower-income. The latter would be the first beneficiaries of any aid. Convinced that this was a worthy conduit for obtaining more immediate assistance to people in need, I called my wife Lisa, explained the situation, and asked her to start networking a fundraising effort for the church. She had the good idea of asking a friend of ours, who is a member of the Christ United Methodist Church in Fort Collins, to approach their pastor about setting up a sister-church relationship to help with fundraising for them. She jumped right on it and over the next week reported progress to me during our daily phone conversations.

I was also able to make headway on travel arrangements to Atlanta for Vinh. Ruth, the generous volunteer in southern Georgia, really did all of the work. I don't know if she was able to secure a donation or discount from Air Tran Airlines, if she raised donations from friends, and/or if she donated money herself, but however she did it, she arranged for Vinh's airfare from Gulfport directly to Atlanta. The only hitch seemed to be that I would need to escort Vinh through security at the Gulfport Airport since he had lost all of his identification in the hurricane. Ruth said that he would be documented in the airline's computers as a hurricane evacuee, which should expedite the process. Another minor hurdle was the fact that the typical Red Cross policy was to not transport clients in Red Cross vehicles for liability and other reasons. This problem struck me as a good situation for applying the guiding principle of "using good judgment and doing what needed to be done, rather than going strictly by policy." During the course of my several phone conversations with Ruth, I happened to mention some of my frustration with the short notice and lack of communication regarding our shelter closing, and its potential impact on the clients. At this point, I had incorrectly assumed that Ruth was a Red Cross volunteer, rather than an independent volunteer, and that I was only venting a bit of frustration to a knowing comrade. The next day I would regret doing so.

Another non-Red Cross opportunity to help out came in the form of a phone call from Dave, a friend in the Kansas City area who is a doctor at a Veterans Administration hospital. He began by saying, "We have about 20 beds in our domiciliary that could potentially be used for veterans in the Mississippi coast area, if they want to relocate. We could provide a broad range of medical support, along with substance abuse counseling and treatment." Dave wondered if I could help him locate the right person to talk with within the V.A. system and on the Mississippi coast. It seemed like a great idea to me, so I told him I'd work on it. Without too much difficulty, and only two or three phone calls, I was able to speak with a doctor at the Biloxi V.A. Hospital, who seemed to be the right person to hook up with Dave. I gave each of them the other's phone number and left it to them to see if they could work something out. Having previously worked in a position with the federal government and knowing of the bureaucratic challenges of such a system, I had my doubts but stayed hopeful.

While I was out in the front parking lot talking with Dave on my cell phone, I noticed that a small group of medical staff, including Carrie, had just arrived and was entering the school. It pleased me that I would now have a chance to catch up on how her volunteer experience was going, and to share email addresses for future correspondence. Unfortunately, by the time I finished my phone call and dealt with a couple of other urgent issues, Carrie and her medical associates had left. Apparently they were engaged in some type of survey of the medical staffing at various shelters. That was the last time that I saw Carrie.

A construction worker, in his late 40's, registered to stay at our shelter during the mid-day. With a very distraught voice, he told me, "It's bad enough that I lost just about everything I own. It's even worse to think of myself as being homeless. I've never needed any assistance or handouts from the government or agencies before, but I just don't see how I can make it without some help now." I tried to comfort him by saying, "There's no shame in accepting some help in a situation like this. You can pay it back in some way in the future when you're back on your feet." I thought that he might want to talk more about his experience with the hurricane, so I asked him. It turned out to be another in a series of dramatic stories of survival. "It was a good thing that I work in construction, because that helped me to know how best to get out of my apartment. I ended up kicking out the sheetrock of two interior walls before I was able to get to a back porch and jump into the water and swim away. I would have been trapped and drowned in my apartment if it weren't for that."

While going for a run on this Thursday, I thought about the work that I was doing. On one hand, it seemed that I was accomplishing a lot or at least I should be, given the long days and the critical needs that we were addressing. On the other hand, my work seemed completely futile, given the massive scale of the need along the entire coast and in New Orleans. With my background in horticulture, I thought of the analogy of manually planting one seed at a time, placing each carefully in the soil and tamping the soil around it, but then looking up and seeing that thousands of unplanted acres stretched to the horizon.

A small bus arrived in the afternoon, carrying about ten teenagers from a church group in the Atlanta area. They had driven the 375 miles to Gulfport specifically to hand out gifts to children in shelters. They had dozens of boxes, shoebox-size and larger, each identified with the word "boy" or "girl." At first, they were just going to hand us the boxes, but I suggested, "Why don't you come inside and hand out the presents yourselves?" They did not need any more persuading. I think the teenagers enjoyed seeing the happy and smiling faces as much as the seven or eight children enjoyed receiving the gifts. Another touching moment came when I was visiting with one of the few children in our shelter, a ten-year-old boy named Jason. I told him that I had a ten-year-old boy named Austin. Jason immediately responded by finding a small radio from a pile of donated items for children and telling me, "I want you to give this to Austin. He'll like it!" On a few other occasions, Jason would greet me with a hug around my waist, reminding me of being home with my family.

On this day of so many rich experiences, I was fortunate to spend more time with Otis. Otis was one of our clients, an older black gentleman with a slim build on a tall frame, who had grown up in New Orleans. Through this conversation and additional ones in the coming days, I found him to be extraordinarily gifted. He was quite intelligent and articulate, but with little formal education, I gathered. He had gone to school with the Neville Brothers of rhythm and blues musical fame, had spent a lot of time at the Apollo theatre in Harlem, and was the most musically-knowledgeable person that I have ever met, most of it gained first-hand. Otis could tell stories for hours on end, intertwining the names of all sorts of famous blues, rhythm and blues, and jazz musicians, without it seeming like name-dropping in the least. He had worked as a disc jockey at one time, and I could imagine him as being a very entertaining person to be interviewed for a radio or television special on the subject of American music. Over the next week, he recommended that I become more familiar with the music of Nena Simone, Soloman Burke, and DJ Rodski.

Otis's cultural knowledge was not limited to music. Sam, another volunteer, later told me that Otis seemingly knew the name of every major league baseball player, past and present. With his ability to wordsmith, Otis also had a repertoire of about 40 self-written poems in his head, many of them quite long. He mentioned that he had a long-held idea of writing up a collection of his poems, and calling it *Thirty Poems and Hope*. I don't know how we got off on the topic of his poetry, but the first one he delivered (he didn't like the word *recited*) for me was "The Peanut Man," a glowing tribute that he wrote about President Carter after he met him in the 1980s. When Otis delivered a poem, he would personalize it by adding the listener's name to the end of an occasional line, giving the impression that he was talking directly to him or her, extemporaneously. He would also gesture broadly with his hands, in a sort of rap style, but modified because he was probably at least 60 years old. Otis would gradually glide around me in a counter-clockwise rotation as he delivered his poem, meaning that I would have to match his pace and rotate with him, to keep him in front of me.

Later in the day I told Otis, "I've been thinking about possible gifts to take home for my two sons. Something that would be real meaningful to me would be if I could hire you to write down a poem about children, so that I could give that to them." I was cautious in asking him not knowing how he would respond to my offer. He seemed receptive and replied, "You know, I've already composed a poem about children." Otis immediately delivered it, and I thought it was beautiful. "I could deliver it again slowly, and you could write it down," Otis suggested. "I'd prefer it in your handwriting," I said, and he understood the significance of that. I got a piece of paper and a pen for him, and Otis went off to the auditorium to remove himself from distractions. About 15 minutes later he came back with the poem written on paper. Uncertain about an appropriate amount to pay him, I was torn between wanting to help him out financially and not offending him with a "handout." "Would $20.00 be reasonable?" I asked. Otis said, "Yes," and graciously accepted it. He told me that it was the first time that he had ever written down one of his poems, and the first time that he had ever been paid for his poetry.

I think there is a strong inclination for many people to want to see the destructive aftermath of a storm. Far more than just the dramatic aspect of it, it is also a way to experience and commune with nature (or God, if you will) in a more direct manner, albeit hardly like watching a sunset over the Grand Canyon. Of course, when destruction occurs at the expense of people's homes, belongings and even lives, it adds a very tragic and sensitive element. During the days and weeks after the Spring Creek flood, I recall being more than a little miffed about the people who would drive slowly down our street, gawking at the destruction as if our neighborhood were a spectacle for their ghoulish entertainment. So, while I had the compelling urge to see some of the worst of the destruction first-hand, I wanted to do it where I wouldn't be seen by the business owners, homeowners, and renters who had suffered. Alternatively, it seemed acceptable to me to witness some of the damage if it were in the context of doing Red Cross work. The most probable opportunity in that realm was with driving through the nearby neighborhoods to distribute any left-over dinners, which we did on most evenings. This activity was very popular with our volunteers because it gave them a chance to get away from the shelter and give meals to people who were extremely appreciative to receive them. It never worked out for me, however, to hand out dinners because more pressing needs at the shelter always prevailed.

I did, though, have four instances of being able to see some of the most heavily-damaged areas. On one occasion, I was going for a run and happened upon a place to cross to the other side of the railroad tracks without being observed by the National Guard. In two other instances I was doing Red Cross errands that necessitated my driving in areas hard hit.

The fourth instance occurred this evening, just as the sun was about to set. George suggested that he and I take a 30-minute break to drive to the beach and count it as our day off. Actually, in addition to my desire to see some of the destruction, I had a yearning to get at least a brief view of the Gulf of Mexico. It would have been disappointing to have traveled 1,300 miles to the Gulf coast and not even see the ocean. George had a similar urge. So, George had me drive and we proceeded to U.S. Highway 49, the main north/south drag through downtown and to the beach. Within one-half mile, two National Guardsmen with their vehicles blocked further access, serving as a checkpoint to keep out potential looters and others without approved business there. As we approached, I could see that few vehicles were in front of us or behind us, most having turned off previously. The handful that did reach the National Guardsmen was being turned around.

It should be mentioned that we were not in a vehicle with a Red Cross placard on it, as George had somewhat mysteriously acquired this vehicle on his own. I imagined that he just got fed up with there not being enough official Red Cross vehicles to complete all of the errands, so he rented it on his own. If we had been in a vehicle identified as being with the Red Cross, they likely would just wave us on. But since we weren't, I asked George, "Do you have any suggestions for what our appeal to the Guardsmen should be?" Seeing their weapons and not wanting to be associated with a painful or embarrassing headline, we decided to go with the straight-ahead and honest approach. We pulled up alongside the Guardsmen, and I rolled down my window. Without saying a word, he looked at me for my explanation. I told him, "We're managers of a Red Cross shelter, and we just wanted to get a quick look at the area along the beach." Simple and to the point. The one Guardsman looked at the other, who must have had seniority. He rolled his eyes, gave a look of perturbed exasperation, and said with military authority, "Okay, but make it quick."

The transition from buildings that were moderately damaged to those that were completely devastated occurred within a relatively short distance. In the downtown area many of the buildings closer to the beach were only shells. Then, along what used to be U.S. 90, which ran right along the hundred-yard-wide beach, the devastation was catastrophic. It was here that the full power of 25-foot-high, tsunami-like waves had hit. Tractor trailer trucks had been tumbled multiple times so that their paint was mostly removed. We saw a few of the casinos, which had previously been anchored just beyond the beach, now iron skeletons several hundred yards inland. One of these was the Grand Casino Gulfport. Six days later, explosives would be detonated to implode it as part of its demolition. With the darkness of late evening, not many people or vehicles were around, and those people we did see were contractors. So, I didn't feel that our gawking and taking a few photos was inconsiderate. Still, I felt that I was being irreverent in some way, knowing that people had lost their lives in this area. About 15 minutes of this activity was enough. We drove back to the shelter, talking about other things.

One of the many destroyed casinos

That evening I heard about a shower truck with hot, potable water operated by the North Carolina Baptist Men's Disaster Relief group, the same group that was preparing our hot meals. It was only a mile or two away, and I jumped at the offer by a Red Cross staffer who was driving a few people over there. Red Cross vehicles were very limited, so it was a real privilege to be able to go there every few days. It was referred to as "getting some air," since we didn't want our 90 or so clients to know that we had this luxury separate from them. I was extremely impressed with this Christian relief organization, and the incredible job they were doing. They were set up in a vacated shopping center parking lot, with dozens of semi-truck trailers that held their food and other supplies. They were completely self-supported with everything that they needed to prepare 8,000 hot meals a day, wash dishes, do laundry, offer showers, and make ice. Nearly 300 men and women staffed the operations, all identified with yellow t-shirts and their group's name. Three and one-half months after returning home, I logged on to their website and discovered some amazing statistics. During their four and one-half months of relief work for Hurricane Katrina, the North Carolina Baptist Men's Disaster Relief group had contributed 45,800 volunteer days of work (equating to an average of 340 men and women working each of those days). Their accomplishments included preparing 524,000 meals, delivering 40 tractor trailer loads of bottled water and supplies, providing emergency childcare for 560 children, producing and donating uncounted tons of ice, and providing the luxury of countless hundreds of showers for appreciative Red Cross volunteers. At that time, with the emergency relief effort winding down and the recovery and rebuilding phases underway, the group had added a new commitment of rebuilding 500 homes in Gulfport over the next two years.[1] During my time in Gulfport, I gained much respect and appreciation for how important this and other private (Christian and otherwise) groups were to the relief effort. In many ways they complemented what the Red Cross and federal government were doing, being more responsive and flexible with meeting immediate needs, and certainly less bureaucratic.

As I was walking out of the shower trailer, I noticed a few people pointing to a jet taking off from the nearby National Guard airstrip. It was Air Force One, presumably with President Bush aboard. The minimal amount of attention that it drew was notable. It was not out of disrespect, but rather a function of everyone being so focused on the work at hand and the fact that this was at least the third time that Air Force One had used the airstrip over the previous several weeks.

Over the course of the ten days that I was a shelter assistant manager, I remember six instances of a staff member finding drug paraphernalia related to crack, methamphetamine, and heroine use, or a client reporting suspected drug use. Drug use was clearly against our policy for living in the shelter, and it was prohibited on our list of rules in the front of the shelter. However, since we never directly caught someone in the act of using drugs, it tended to become overshadowed by more pressing issues.

One of our most scary clients was Jeff. He wasn't threatening with his physical size, being only about 5' 8" and somewhat thin. What was frightening about him was his state of mind. Jeff wore dark sunglasses—even inside the building—and would stare straight ahead with an extremely mean look on his face. Our mental health worker described him as psychotic, which he very well may have been. He also had an impolite nature. I once tried to engage him with, "Hello, how're you doing?", and he responded with a distinctly unfriendly, "Get the f___ out of my way." He was frightening enough to several staff members and clients that we had the police talk with him. Jeff started out by being belligerent, but that didn't last long. They used their own particular style of "tough love" on him, which seemed to turn him around a little.

A small selection of employment opportunities was available for our clients, if they had the health and fitness to be able to do manual labor in the hot sun. On our informal bulletin board were several notices for day laborers to assist with the cleanup of buildings and yards, paying $8.00 to $10.00 per hour. At least one pickup truck would arrive early each morning to transport any willing workers to the work sites. Five to ten of our clients would typically take advantage of that financial opportunity.

After such a full and eventful day, it took awhile to unwind enough to fall asleep. While lying on my cot, I thought about the contrast between a normal day in my life and the day that I had just completed. While my typical days are by no means predictable and stale, they are definitely no match for the variety, stimulation, and sense of adventure I was experiencing in Gulfport. Although I do not mind a small degree of routine in life, even finding solace and grounding in it, I start feeling confined and stunted when it reaches the predictable category. In fact, I take certain actions to shake up my tendency towards routine, to remind me of my need for and joy of spontaneity. For example, I happened to observe one day that I always parked in the same general area of my workplace parking lot, closest to the building. No big deal, in the overall scheme of things, but it struck me as being symbolic of mindless routine. Since that realization, I now intentionally vary my parking location, even though not in the closest spots available. That eccentric little action—which I dub intentional symbolic spontaneity—is enough to remind me at the start of the day to have an open and fresh attitude towards life and whatever it brings. No such symbolic actions were needed at the shelter, as each day was anything but routine.

### Friday, September 16

*In a national address from New Orleans last evening, President Bush promised that the government would pay for most of the costs of rebuilding the hurricane-ravaged*

*Gulf Coast in one of the largest reconstruction projects the world has ever seen. "There is no way to imagine America without New Orleans, and this great city will rise again," the president said. The government's cost for rebuilding could reach $200 billion or beyond. Earlier in the day, Bush spent time in Gulfport and other Mississippi coast communities, discussing the recovery effort.*

Although not feeling anything close to what you could call well-rested, I woke at the usual time of 6:30-ish, grabbed a five-minute breakfast and wandered around the inside of the school to check on things. A while later, I found George in the manager's office, having recently phoned in his morning report, provided our order for any needed supplies and the number of clients that we had the previous night (accomplished by one of the night staff counting people when they were asleep at around 2:00 a.m.). Of course, George asked the supervisor if she knew where we would be moving tomorrow, but the best she could do was to provide a list of five possibilities.

One of my more interesting visits on this day was with a white woman, Amy, who came with her eleven-year-old son, Wilson, to check on the status of the school. Under more normal circumstances, I would have described Amy as looking exhausted and distraught, but that would be a meaningless description in this setting, since nearly every one of the people I met looked that way. While chatting with her, I learned that Wilson was her ninth child, a startling fact not only for the monumental achievement of having nine children but more so because she didn't look to be older than 35. Obviously, I didn't say anything or ask personal questions because it was none of my business, but I couldn't stop myself from doing the math and trying to figure out how she could have had eight children older than Wilson, when she was so young. I concluded that there had to be step-children as part of the mixture. At any rate, she struck me as a very caring and attentive parent.

Her usual employment was as a long-haul truck driver. I asked Amy about her and Wilson's experience with the hurricane. She answered matter-of-factly, "The water came up real fast and we had to swim for our lives. I was very proud of Wilson. I'm not sure I could have kept him above water on my own if he didn't know how to swim." With enthusiasm and an air of accomplishment, Wilson added, "It's a good thing I took swimming lessons. I would have died if I didn't." He expressed no fear or grief in relating his experience. It was as if he were telling me about something as simple and common as attaining a good grade on a test or hitting a home run.

With our anticipated move coming the next day, an ever-expanding pile of trash on the grounds, and frustration at many of the clients' laziness and sloppiness, Lucy, the head of the nursing staff, decided to use a drill sergeant approach to recruit the clients to help. For the most part, I agreed with her assessment and shared her frustration, but I knew this approach was destined for failure. She started at the end of the hall and marched toward the front of the building, firmly demanding that the clients get off their duffs and go outside to help. Some of them looked at her with amusement, others a blank stare, and the rest completely ignored her. She seemed to become more and more upset as she realized the futility of it. I would guess that about 30 clients heard her aggressive pleading, with a grand total of one client following her out to the trash pile.

On more than one occasion I thought about the unfathomable amount of debris and trash generated by this hurricane and all of its ramifications. To begin with, it's difficult to even conceive of the gargantuan weight and volume of the waste that would be generated from the building materials and contents of thousands of destroyed and damaged homes, along with countless thousands of downed trees and limbs, then to think of the time, cost, and labor required to load and transport all of that debris. However, given more thought, all of those steps—as daunting as they are—would be further complicated by the fact that any one debris pile could easily contain everything from lumber, to furniture, to appliances, to hazardous household waste, to valuable mementos, with some of those materials salvageable and much of it not. To be removed with the least environmental impact, all of the debris would need to be assessed and sorted, and then delivered to its respective location. Lastly, how does the material considered to be non-salvageable get disposed? Buried? Imagine the landfill area and volume required for doing so. Burned? What are the air quality consequences of that approach? Also, the amount of trash generated from the relief effort itself was notable. As near as I could estimate, each of our 100 or so volunteers and clients was generating one-fourth to one-half of a large trash bag per day. Multiply that by the hundreds of thousands of volunteers and clients, over many days or weeks, and you arrive at a mammoth pile of refuse. The vast majority of this waste was due to virtually all of our food and beverages being delivered and consumed in containers. Each meal was served in a Styrofoam clam-shell, along with plastic utensils and drinks contained in aluminum cans, plastic cups, or plastic bottles. Of course, there was no reasonable alternative to this throw-away approach because we did not have the capacity to wash dishes and utensils. Yet another layer of impact—the generation of colossal amounts of debris and trash, with the associated environmental consequences—caused by this monumental disaster.

During the morning I received a phone call on my cell phone from Ruth. I felt a blip of panic when Ruth informed me, "I was so upset about the Red Cross shutting down your shelter and throwing needy people out in the street that I called a friend who is the manager of a Jacksonville television station. I asked her to do some investigative reporting." Ruth genuinely felt that she was helping out by doing so. "Oh great," I thought sarcastically. I imagined the personal fallout that would result from that one. While silently cursing myself for my poor judgment in previously sharing that with her, I quickly clarified the situation for her. It was *not* accurate to say that the Red Cross was closing a shelter, and to leave it at that. Furthermore, it was *completely* inaccurate to say that we (the Red Cross) were throwing our clients out in the street. Yes, this shelter was closing because the school district needed to prepare it for re-opening as a school, but the clients would all be given the option, with transportation provided, to move to another shelter. I apologized for my misinforming her, expressed my appreciation for her concern about the clients' welfare, and asked that she call her friend to correct the situation. Either Ruth made the corrective phone call or her friend never pursued Ruth's tip, as there was no repercussion that I heard about.

On this Friday, I noticed how much a few simple words of thanks or gratitude could make a difference in my attitude and spirit. I have several distinct memories of staff members or clients sending such kindness my way. My favorite phrase was from a black woman who responded to my helping someone by saying, "The Lord's gonna bless you for that." The expression of gratitude that I least expected was from a Verizon Wireless representative headquartered in some other state. I was talking with him about my situation as a Red Cross volunteer making a lot of calls, and that I needed to upgrade my plan to more minutes to prevent overcharges. He ended the conversation by saying very sincerely, "Thank you for what you're doing." It demonstrated the degree to which this was a national tragedy, when what would otherwise be a business-like exchange of information with a nameless stranger sitting in an office in some distant state would now end as a personal and caring conversation. These compliments and other kind words were more than enough to offset annoyances that left me shaking my head, such as a vehement complaint about the flavor of Vienna sausages that we had as a snack choice and a demand that we open up an M.R.E., just so the client could pull out his favorite flavor of tea and pitch the rest of it.

At any one moment, I could easily think of at least a dozen tasks that I could do to fulfill my general objective of helping with the relief effort. The most humdrum level included many routine things that needed to be done to keep the shelter operating, whether taking out trash, re-filling the ice in the ice chests, helping to serve food, or setting up a client with a cot. The next higher category consisted of activities that would have a little more impact, such as engaging in a supportive conversation with a staff member or client or taking a person with an injury or illness to the nurses' office. At the highest grouping were actions that I could take to dramatically improve the life of one or more people, sometimes with a few simple phone calls or a bit of creative problem-solving. I was continually trying to keep this array of tasks in balance, since a number of the routine things simply had to get done, but I always leaned towards the two higher levels when there was a choice.

Many of the staff members wanted to change their return flight schedules, now that they were down in Gulfport, a four-hour drive from Montgomery where most of us originally landed. While it was possible to catch a Red Cross shuttle back up to Montgomery, there was only one shuttle per day, so it would save a lot of time to be able to fly out of Gulfport or Mobile, Alabama, 40 miles away. Unfortunately, any travel changes had to go through BTI, the travel agency contracted with the Red Cross, and it was often very difficult to get through to them. Dawn ended up tackling this task for most of the staff. She was often limited with her cell phone's reception, and getting through out of the Gulfport area. Dawn discovered that it was more effective to arrange for the local Red Cross office from the volunteer's home location to make the call, so she helped initiate that process. Good problem-solving on Dawn's part, as we had come to expect from her! Another attribute of Dawn's was her compassion for animals. From early on, some of the staff members became aware of a dog that was chained up in the backyard of a home across the alley from the school. The occupants had apparently evacuated before the hurricane, leaving the dog to fend for itself. The neighbor woman had taken pity on it, keeping it fed and watered. The dog was not in good health, though, and had an infected wound. With the involvement of the neighbor woman, Dawn was able to have the dog transported to an animal shelter, where it would be put on a list to receive veterinary care. It would eventually be put up for adoption, assuming the owners did not return for it.

At noon, a woman being assisted by another person gingerly walked into our shelter. She had the classic appearance of an advanced case of hepatitis A, with noticeably yellow skin and yellow sclera, the "whites" of her eyes. She said that she had contracted the disease from a dog bite. As if that wasn't enough, she was also extremely dehydrated. The medical staff immediately attended to her, and she registered to stay.

During the past week, I had heard local radio broadcasts several times, once while running an errand in the car and a few times over-hearing clients' radios in the shelter. The formats of the stations varied—talk radio, Christian, and black gospel—but in all cases the content focused on the hurricane relief with an uplifting and encouraging spin. Whether news about where people could receive relief services, an interview with a FEMA representative, or a few inspirational words in between music, the disc jockeys all expressed a "We can get through this!" message to their listeners.

At this mid-point of my two-week deployment, I still firmly believed that I had been divinely led to serve with this relief mission. By no means was this a feeling of grandiosity—that I was destined to perform some heroic act or make a huge difference. Rather, it was simply an unwavering conviction that I was listening to my heart and following the guidance that life was presenting me, not necessarily knowing where it would lead. This feeling was a remarkable change for me. Previous to this recently-initiated phase of my search for purpose, my personal belief system had been that free will and chance play a much larger role in people's lives than God's will (determinism, providence, fate, grace…whatever you would like to call it). It's not that I thought that humans have more power than our Supreme Being, quite the contrary. It just seemed that God would have better things to do than dink around with who I would meet on a particular day, for example. More recently though, I had been feeling a much stronger sense of God's presence in my day-to-day life, and how that spiritual light can move through human action if we're open to it. I thought of it as a slowly manifesting epiphany.

Because of the length and intensity of each day's work, I did not have the luxury of pondering the spiritual big picture of my experience, so I had not yet ascertained messages and lessons from a Higher Power. That examination would have to wait until I returned home. I do not mean that I did not feel spiritually connected while engaged in my daily duties and encounters. On many occasions I most definitely did, typically through intimate conversations with hurricane victims.

If I were to identify one particular encounter—one instance of crossing paths with another person—that gave me the greatest confirmation of my having answered a calling, then it would be meeting Anna on this day. I first noticed her when she was in the shelter's entry area, near the registration desk. In the midst of an assortment of other happenings and people all about, she was talking with a younger Red Cross volunteer, and her eyes were tearing up. The volunteer looked as if she wasn't certain how to handle the situation, so I tried to ease in, without wanting to be intrusive. Anna seemed receptive to my listening, and the volunteer slipped away to take on some other task. It was not the least bit uncommon for us to have people crying in our shelter, so other people may not have really even noticed, but I thought Anna might be more comfortable with a bit of privacy, so I suggested we go sit in the auditorium. A dozen or more clients were in there, but they were spread around and focused on their own activities.

Anna began to share her pain with her loses associated with the hurricane. Our conversation transitioned to her difficult upbringing. "I was adopted and raised by my mother, who was a Pentecostal preacher…and also an alcoholic. I was born with fetal alcohol syndrome, before they had a name for it." Through our visiting, I gathered that Anna never had a father; only boyfriends of her mother that would change every two or three years. She didn't know the exact number or whereabouts of all of her siblings, half-siblings, and step-siblings. "I starting drinking and doing drugs when I was 11," Anna told me. She was wiping tears from her face, and I guess that I finally had reached my limit for hearing—and feeling—painful stories over the past week. Thus far I had been able to listen to stories with empathy but still keep detached enough to not become overwhelmed by them. But this time, perhaps my 20th instance of listening to a person express his or her pain and grief, I couldn't hold back some tears. "Are you okay?" she asked, surprised at my reaction. I replied by saying, "It's just the accumulation of hearing so much pain and feeling frustrated about not being able to do more to help. I'll be fine." As I regained a bit of composure, I recalled with some embarrassment how the Red Cross instructor in Montgomery had advised us to keep our emotions in check, emphasizing that the last thing someone grieving needed was a person in the role of supporting them to be overcome with his own emotion.

What was most revealing to me about Anna, as she shared her story, was not the content. Although it most certainly struck me that I was in the presence of a woman who had been through a very painful upbringing, the more profound feeling was of being in the presence of a woman who was a shining light of positive spirit. Her voice or manner did not indicate even a shred of self-pity or desire on her part for sympathy. To the contrary, she shared her story in a way that caused me to think of her as being still fully aware of her past, but having grown above and beyond it with a higher perspective. It was still a part of her and it always would be, but she was speaking about it from a position of spiritual strength. Therefore I was not the least bit surprised to hear her say that through a strong support group, prayer, and a deep relationship with a Higher Power, she had now been clean and sober for two and one-half years.

Anna had been with her support group when they sought shelter from the approaching hurricane in the flimsy metal building that served as their usual meeting place. In describing her experience she said, "The wind and driving rain kept getting stronger and louder, to the point that you couldn't hear someone yelling in the same room. We held hands and prayed for our survival. Even though it was daylight, it was almost as dark as night, with the torrential rain and clouds. When I looked out a window, with the flashes of lightning you could see road signs, sections of roofing, and huge pieces of metal siding fly by like pieces of paper." There was a look in Anna's eyes that expressed the intensity of her experience. She continued by saying, "When the storm finally stopped we walked out of our building and were amazed to see downed trees and mostly flattened buildings in every direction. Many of those buildings were much more sturdily built than the one we were in, but ours had minimal damage."

For the second time while in Gulfport, I decided to introduce cautiously the idea of providing assistance for someone to relocate to Fort Collins. I'm not sure why I did so, as she had not led me to believe that she wanted to move from Gulfport. Perhaps it was nothing more than my reaction to help her in the most dramatic way that I could personally offer. Or, perhaps there was some spiritual force at play, and I was a conduit. She expressed interest, but would obviously need to give it some thought. I don't know that either of us was aware of it at the time, but this crossing of paths—whether a simple "roll of the dice" or divine involvement—would end up changing both of our lives in major ways.

This also was to be the day to take Vinh to the Gulfport airport. I had previously arranged with George to use his vehicle to transport Vinh. Someone had donated a fairly high quality bicycle to him a week prior, so that he could get around Gulfport. He obviously couldn't take it on the plane, and he was happy to leave it at the shelter for whoever needed it. During the short ten-minute drive to the airport, he talked more about his background and about his experience during the hurricane. With it being a very small airport, the check-in process was quick, and there was no problem with explaining Vinh's situation. I had my Red Cross vest on, just in case it was needed to verify my position and vouch for Vinh's story. The security gate was within 40 feet of the ticket counter, so the counter employee simply walked over with us to the security officer to allow his admittance without identification. And with that, Vinh and I exchanged a warm handshake and he was off to Atlanta. I'm not sure that I have ever seen a bigger smile.

Later in the afternoon, I noticed in our parking lot a middle-aged woman who had just gotten out of her S.U.V. She was talking with one of our staff, with tears rolling down her face. I approached to see if I could help. Through her crying she told me, "My house is in ruins and I've been sleeping on a pallet. I only have $32, but I'm wondering if it's enough to buy a cot." I was pretty sure that the typical Red Cross policy would not allow selling or giving away cots, but I didn't want to ask to find out. I also didn't want to create a scene in the front of the shelter by bringing a cot out, so I told her, "Why don't you drive around to the back of the gym on the north side. I'll meet you there." I grabbed one of the hundreds that we had stored in boxes in the gym, took it out the gym door and loaded it in her car. Still crying, she tried to hand me the $32, but I wouldn't accept it. I told her that I would purchase the cot and make it a personal donation if I needed to. She thanked me profusely and drove off.

An older white gentleman by the name of Johnny showed up that day, desperately looking for his wife and daughter. By his behavior, we thought that he might have Alzheimer's, and we weren't sure if he actually had a wife and daughter. In fact, the next day he wandered away from the shelter, causing some concern on the part of the staff, before he was found a few blocks away. After two days of looking through lists of "found" persons and calling other shelters as they had time, our staff still had no answer for Johnny. Then miraculously, the previously-mentioned Anna (who happened to be a friend of Johnny's) was able to locate his family in a Gulfport apartment and re-unite them.

While I was cleaning out one of the bathrooms, several of us smelled smoke. We traced it to the bathroom across the hall and found some smoldering papers in one of the toilet stalls. Curiously, the door was locked with no one in the stall, meaning that the person would have had to crawl under the door to exit. We suspected and later confirmed that it was Jacob, a seven-year-old boy who had a very active fascination with fire. Someone else told us that he had been obtaining the matches from M.R.E.'s. It was time to start keeping closer tabs on the M.R.E.'s—and Jacob.

Towards the end of the evening, a quickly arranged talent show was held in the auditorium. Not many people attended—maybe 10 staff members and 20 clients—but it was a neat thing to do. Jeremy sang and played the guitar, while Trevor just kind of hung out on the stage with him, including calling a friend on his cell phone so that the friend could hear Jeremy sing. A few of the young-adult clients did some quasi-Karaoke while their portly, seven-year-old son attempted to break dance. For those who attended it brought a small degree of closure to their time spent at the Gulfport Central Elementary School shelter, on this last evening of its service, although that might have been offset by the anxiety of not knowing where they would be relocated to the next day.

While lying on my cot and waiting for sleep to overtake me, I came to the realization that during the previous week I had literally not given one minute of thought to my job back home, my search for a greater sense of purpose, or any other issues and concerns in my "real life." Every bit of my being had been focused on the present, or if it shifted to the past or future it still related to my experience in Gulfport, a reflection not only of the intensity of my time there, but also of how I had the sense of being "in the flow," or "in a zone," to borrow current sports terminology. It had many of the same defining characteristics, such as feeling detached from time and a sense of self, and performing at a peak level. Many "finding your mission" type of books suggest identifying just such experiences in one's life, as an indication of being aligned with skills, interests, and values. And with that thought, my mind did jump beyond Gulfport to the topic of my ongoing search for purpose, trying to identify qualities of my recent experience that might be replicated in other settings and vocational pursuits. I did not get very far before I succumbed to sleep.

### Saturday, September 17

*An article in the Gulfport SunHerald reported on Katrina's devastating impact on nearby Biloxi's shrimping industry, largely run by Vietnamese immigrants. In the mid 70's, Vietnamese immigrants poured into the Gulf Coast from Texas to Florida and began shrimping. They bought small boats, then bigger ones, and became successful. Locals unaccustomed to the competition occasionally struck back with violence. The Vietnamese stayed firm and became more rooted in the community. When Katrina approached, most of the Vietnamese shrimpers rode out the storm on their boats—worth up to $700,000 apiece—huddled in a canal deep inside Biloxi's Back Bay, often with their families aboard. It proved to be inadequate protection, as 25 to 30 of the boats were destroyed, about one-quarter of Biloxi's entire fleet. At least 11 people died on the boats, including two children.*

George called in his daily report at 7:30 a.m. We were told that we were going to the Good Deeds Community Center, four or five miles away. A bus would arrive at about 9:00 a.m. to start transporting our clients, and a truck would follow up soon after that to carry all of the clients' belongings. George promptly headed to the flip chart sign with his Sharpie pen, and we began spreading the word.

To say that there was a negative reaction to this news would be an understatement. Evidently, this particular part of town did not have a stellar reputation. One client told me, "I'm a street person, and I think it's too dangerous to go there." Another was heard to say, "We're moving from a neighborhood of crack users to a neighborhood of crack producers." Stories alluding to extensive gang activity and a proliferation of weapons caused some concern, but we had learned to take everything that we heard with a grain of salt, regardless of the source. Still, we thought it prudent to send about four of our staff members over to the Good Deeds shelter to do a reconnaissance and to start setting it up. (With the prevalence of misinformation and hearsay, jumping in a vehicle and doing an in-person scouting mission was often the best method for obtaining accurate information.) We had heard that there was a volunteer by the name of Henry who was going to be the manager of this shelter, but we didn't know if he was already there or if he had any staff with him, nor did we have any way of contacting him.

In addition to the safety concern, our clients who were about to be picked up to put in a day's worth of manual work were concerned about what they should do with their belongings. They would have to trust that we would safely deliver their piles of boxed and bagged possessions to the new shelter, and that we would have a bus at the school shelter to transport them when they returned.

The bus arrived and the exodus began. The first load of eight clients took their belongings with them, understandably not wanting to be separated from them. When the bus driver returned about 30 minutes later to take the next group of passengers, he told us that his supervisor would not allow the belongings on the bus, and that the truck would have to be used for that purpose. The clients were in various stages of preparation. Some had their piles of possessions on the front walk, writing their names on the bags and boxes. Others were inside trying to gather up their stuff. Many others had not even begun, and there was a tremendous mass of belongings still scattered throughout the hallways and auditorium. It was obvious that our staff would end up having to deal with a lot of it, and it would be difficult to discern between outright trash and people's treasures. We started out with what was obviously trash, lugging out many dozens of full trash bags.

In the midst of this activity, a woman standing beside a car in the parking lot saw my Red Cross vest and motioned for me to come over. In a somewhat hushed tone, she explained, "I was just approached by one of your clients, who asked me to give him a ride to a nearby address. I want to be helpful, but I don't even know the guy so I'm wondering if you can help me. Can you write down your name and cell phone number, so I have it in case he does something I don't like?"

I responded by saying, "Can you tell me who it is that asked you for the ride?"

Without directly pointing, she described where I could see him over to the side of the parking lot. It was Leroy, a suspected drug user who had previously caused some concern.

"I don't think you should take a chance on him. He can walk if he needs to get somewhere," I warned.

She was insistent, so I gave her my cell phone number and also wrote down her cell phone number and her license plate number. She left with Leroy, and I nervously waited for about ten minutes and then called her. "I just dropped him off and everything's fine. Thanks for checking," she said.

It was at about that time that one of our clients (who happened to have a vehicle at the shelter) returned from checking out the Good Deeds shelter. He was concerned after hearing the stories about it and had wanted to check it out for himself. With his alarming report he said, "We were only able to get a few blocks from the shelter. A huge traffic jam and a mob of upset people kept us from getting any closer. A bunch of armed National Guard troops were trying to get some control. It sure didn't seem safe to me."

That information was the last straw for George and me. We told the bus driver waiting out front to not load up any passengers. We were absolutely not going to proceed if there was any physical risk to our clients or staff. I immediately called Dale, one of the four staff members that we had sent over earlier. Completely contrary to these other reports, he said that everything seemed perfectly fine and calm, and only a few people were there. Obviously, something wasn't matching up. I queried the client who had just returned with the dire assessment about the precise location that he witnessed. As it turned out, he had turned west off of Highway 49 instead of east. We eventually realized that he had observed a location where the Red Cross was distributing checks to hurricane victims rather than the Good Deeds shelter. So, we were back on track for the exodus to Good Deeds.

In the late morning, after about half of our clients and their gear were presumably moved successfully to Good Deeds, we received a phone call from the local Red Cross headquarters. They informed us that, because of additional clients who would be going to Good Deeds from another closing-down shelter, Good

Deeds was now maxed out. Our remaining clients were to go to the Harrison County Skate Park shelter, which was also being set up that day. They also requested that our staff be split up and that George and I should go to the Skate Park with about half of the staff. The remaining half should go to Good Deeds, where Henry would serve as the new manager.

Planning board at Gulfport Red Cross headquarters, indicating the consolidation of shelters

This news was hardly great. First, because the gear was being taken over to Good Deeds in a truck, separate from the bus taking the clients, we now had clients at our school who were supposed to go to the Skate Park but whose belongings were at Good Deeds, including some clients' medications that needed to be taken daily. We weren't certain how well people had identified their bags and boxes of possessions or how orderly they were being stockpiled at Good Deeds. Second, many of these clients had weathered some very traumatic events together and had formed strong bonds. They felt like extended family and did not want to be broken up. Although they did have the choice of which shelter to go to, few had their own transportation to be able to take advantage of that option. Third, for similar reasons, we had hoped to keep our staff together as one unit or at least have the opportunity to say goodbye. Fortunately, a list of the staff members' names, addresses, and emails had already been compiled so that we could contact each other after returning home, if desired. And we all knew that the nature of our job was to serve wherever we were needed.

George told me, "Why don't you head on over to the Skate Park with Carl (the volunteer who did most of the driving and delivery duties) to check things out and to begin to set it up as a shelter. I'll stay here with the remaining staff and make sure everything gets cleaned up." Before doing so, I called Lisa for our daily conversation. I told her about my meeting and experience with Anna the day before and asked that she start networking for lodging for her in the event that she decided to relocate. She immediately had some good ideas for possibilities and was enthusiastic about proceeding.

The Harrison County Skate Park was about three miles to the east of the Gulfport Elementary School, still in Gulfport but within a few blocks of Biloxi. When we arrived, we saw that there was one large metal building that housed the indoor skating rink for in-line hockey. Being far enough inland, it appeared to have sustained only minor damage from the hurricane. A "half-pipe" and other wooden structures for skateboarding stood unused outside the building, within a fenced area. When entering the building, I saw a man working inside, and my attention was immediately drawn to his loose-fitting cotton pants with horizontal green stripes. "That's a rather bizarre style, but to each his own," I thought. Then I noticed about seven other men were spread around the inside of the building, all wearing matching pants. Simultaneously, I read the back of one of the t-shirts, which identified them as Harrison County convicts. From that perspective, the horizontal green stripes didn't seem so bad, certainly not as dowdy as the bright orange color of the inmates' clothing at our local jail. They were helping to prepare the facility to be used as a shelter by covering the entire rink with sections of carpet with an incredible array of colors and naps. You could have done a chronological history of the last 30 years of American carpeting—all the way back to lime green shag—with what was being duct-taped to the floor. Their horizontal green-striped pants actually complemented the carpet quite well.

To be honest, my first thoughts after noticing the convicts were not about their work nor the aesthetic qualities of the floor covering. Seeing the convicts and imagining they were guilty of heinous crimes, my first thoughts were, "Where are the armed guards?" and "Where is the nearest exit for a quick escape?" A man of average height and build was clearly supervising them, but he was conspicuously unarmed. My reaction was a conflicted combination of comfort and concern. I was relieved in thinking that if there was no need for an armed guard, they were probably busted for crimes ranging from jaywalking to littering. On the other hand, I felt apprehension in wondering if they had drastically underestimated the convicts' latent violent tendencies.

Entrance to the Harrison County Skate Park shelter

At about the same time that Carl and I arrived, three Red Cross volunteers from the local headquarters appeared, assigned to check out the building for its suitability as a shelter. I walked around the inside of the building with them so that I could assess it for setting up a manager's office, sleeping quarters for the staff, bathrooms, etc. After about five minutes of looking things over, Kevin, one of the three volunteers from headquarters, had a lengthy list of what was wrong with the building and how it was entirely unacceptable as a shelter. His list included air conditioning that wasn't functioning well, sections of fiberglass insulation hanging from the ceiling of the dressing rooms exposing holes in the metal roof through which you could see daylight, only two toilets per gender, and no showers. As he continued with his negative appraisal, I stopped him and said that I needed to ask him something. I took a deep breath to calm myself down a bit and said, "I realize that you're just doing the job that you were trained for—to assess prospective shelter locations—but we've got a timing issue here. Wouldn't it have made a little more sense to do this assessment *before* the decision was made to set it up as a shelter, and *before* we were told to stop sending clients to the Good Deeds shelter and to send them to this shelter? I could care less if there's insulation falling from the ceiling in the dressing rooms. We'll clean it up, and we'll put a tarp on the roof. We're not going to jerk our clients around again, so why don't we try to focus on what we can do to make this thing work." He muttered something in response and I walked away to begin to unload the supplies that we had brought with us.

In addition to the three Red Cross staff members from the local headquarters and the group of convicts and supervisor, there was also the manager for the Skate Park and three members of the Tallahassee, Florida Emergency Response Team. The latter was volunteering time to assist Harrison County in various emergency response tasks, in this case to set up the shelter.

Sometime during this hyperactivity, a group of soldiers showed up from the local Navy Seabee base. Their objective was to set up something they called a buffalo shower, which was a self-contained shower unit with its own water heater and potable water supply. Next to obtaining some Porta-Toilets, this need was at the top of my list, given that we currently had no showers, we were expecting to have 90 or more people living here within a few days, and it was 95 degrees and about 60% humidity outside, with only two of the four air conditioning units working. They had a trailer-load of all of the lumber, plastic sheeting, and other materials needed to build several of these showers, but decided to take the trailer back with them rather than unload it because it was getting late into the afternoon. "We'll be back tomorrow to build your showers," they told me.

I busied myself with preparing the shelter by cleaning out the four changing rooms (each about 10 feet by 10 feet), that would serve as a nurses' medical room and three staff members' sleeping rooms. No tools were available for doing this cleanup so I had to improvise. A section of metal roofing lying outside of the building turned out to be pretty handy as a scraper to remove the wet ceiling sheetrock that had cemented itself to the floor. I set up a desk and chairs in another small room at the entrance to serve as the manager's office, and I posted some signs to distinguish the uses for different areas of the building.

A while later George called, and we discussed our transition strategy. He and one staffer would stay at the school for another night, so that they could finish up with the cleaning and closeout work. He would soon be sending the other three staff members over to the Skate Park, along with all of the supplies—cots, food, and otherwise—that we thought we might need from the school shelter.

Throughout the afternoon, clients began to filter in, some that we knew from our shelter at Gulfport Central Elementary, and some who were from Ocean Grove Elementary, which also closed this Saturday. Unexpectedly, we were also joined by three new Red Cross staff members from that school.

At about 11:15 p.m., with only about 15 clients now in our shelter and the basics of setting up the shelter accomplished, I turned over the reins to the sheriff's deputy who was pulling the night shift. Before retreating to the sanctity of the ten foot by ten foot locker room with a skylight (a euphemism for the holes in the flat metal roofing above), I followed Lisa's recommendation to acquire some Tylenol PM from the two nurses to overcome my insomnia. They worked well, as I have no memory of thoughts or reflections before drifting off to sleep.

# 5

## *Making the Most of the Last*

*What allows us, as human beings, to psychologically survive life on earth, with all of its pain, drama, and challenges, is a sense of purpose and meaning.*

*—Barbara De Angelis*

**Sunday, September 18**

*The Gulfport SunHerald reported that Bob Hobbs, an 82-year-old diabetic, was trapped on the second floor of his severely damaged home near the Gulfport beach for one week. Temperatures in the home exceeded 100 degrees and he survived on contaminated water. He was rescued by the son of his long-time Navy buddy, who drove 900 miles without rest from Ohio, after being notified by neighbors of Hobbs.*

After my best night's sleep in more than a week, I awoke and went out to get some breakfast. The Skate Park had a small kitchen and concession window, which was perfect for distributing our cold breakfast and snack items. One of our new Red Cross volunteers, Jennifer, had taken on the managing of the kitchen and snack counter, having been previously employed as a restaurant manager in Pennsylvania. She did a superlative job.

One of our other volunteers, Alison, did not work out as well. She was dedicated to helping others but never seemed to grasp the structure of the Red Cross system that she was working within. On this day, before we received an anticipated additional 70 or so clients, we had about a one-to-one ratio of Red Cross staff members to clients. Frustrated with not feeling useful, she told me, "Since it doesn't seem like I'm needed here, I'm thinking of driving with my mom (who happened to live in the area) over to another shelter." Concerned with her statement, I said, "It might be a good idea to rethink that. Even though you and I are volunteers, we still need to work within the Red Cross structure. We can't just be moving around on our own initiative. If we think the over-staffing is going to continue, then we should call the local headquarters and talk with them about the situation. They're telling us we're supposed to receive more clients in the next few days, so how about if we see how that goes?" I could tell my words only partially convinced her.

Our numbers of clients did increase over the next few days, and there was plenty of work to keep all of our staff busy. Alison, along with her mother, settled into helping with the registration desk and serving meals. They performed those tasks admirably. However, when she was asked if she wanted to succeed Dawn in her "executive secretary" position, Alison elected to leave, to where we didn't know.

In the morning, I was handed a written message that a woman from San Diego was looking for her son. The note had her name, her phone number, and her son's name. Looking through our list of registration forms, I found no name that matched her son's. I called her up and told her that he had not registered with us. It would have been great to be able to refer her to a phone number or an email address for a Red Cross headquarters, which could then pass on her request to all of the shelters. Obviously though, without internet hookups and without a system for submitting the names of shelter registrants to the headquarters, that request could not be made. She sounded dejected, and I didn't want to leave her feeling so down. I gave her several website addresses that had been set up to connect "looking" people with "missing" people. Of course, many of the people who were "missing" might not have known that people were looking for them, nor would they have any means to register with such a website.

A reporter from the *Kansas City Star* wandered into the shelter to ask some general questions. He said that he had been in the area for about a week, filing daily dispatches. I told him that I grew up in Overland Park, a suburb of Kansas City, and we talked a bit about the cultural differences between there and the South. One of the many things that I appreciate about the South is the higher degree of manners and respect for other people. I imagine there are some people who would argue that such attitudes are contrived and/or too rigid, but I haven't felt that way in the six or seven weeks that I have spent in the South during the past ten years. I especially like the tradition of addressing people with a combination of the title Mister or Miss and their first name, an exchange done not only between children and adults, but even between adults, especially if not well acquainted. I have had some regret not raising our boys to refer to adult friends of the family with that approach. I could not go so far as to require them to call an adult by "Mr." or "Mrs." and the last name (unless they are clearly older than me), but I also feel some discomfort in their calling adults in their 30's and older just by the first name. I want them to feel comfortable and self-confident around adults, but I also want them to have and show respect for them. The "Mister Rich" or "Miss Barb" approach seems to be a good compromise. But, alas, it's too late now that they are ten and thirteen years old, and they tell me that they would feel very odd and uncomfortable in using those titles in Fort Collins, since it is rarely done in their world.

Since arriving in Gulfport, I had also been reflecting on some racial issues. Gulfport is about 60 percent white, 34 percent black and 6 percent Hispanic, Asian, and other. Because of the neighborhood that our shelter was in and the demographics of the people needing the support, our clients were about 70 percent black and 30 percent white. I have lived in seven cities in Kansas, Oregon, and Colorado, varying in size from 400 to a metropolitan area of over one and one-half million, with the prevalent politics ranging from very conservative to quite progressive. In all cases, however, the black population was either non-existent or nearly so, or the blacks and whites were largely de-facto segregated into their respective sections of the city. I can count on one hand the number of blacks that I have formed acquaintances or friendships with during my entire life, not for a lack of desire, but for the sheer fact that there have been nearly negligible opportunities.

While traveling on the Georgia and South Carolina coasts, and now on the Mississippi coast, I saw much more thorough integration of whites and blacks. Because of the ordinariness of the two races routinely living, working, and socializing together, I have observed a comfort level between the blacks and whites that I had not fully expected. In no way am I denying that there is still bitterness, anger, and racism, in the South and in the rest of the country. I am only saying that, in the world that I live in—which is not uncommon for millions of whites—there is little opportunity to establish relationships with blacks, and because of that, there is an apprehension and tentativeness by a white person who comes to a setting that is predominantly black. My apprehension is born of sensitivity to past injustices wrought by my race and my being not entirely certain about the best way to deal with that. I wonder how much I am viewed as an individual and only judged on *my* words and actions, and how much I am viewed as a representative of my race and all of the associated history. And then there is that thing about the urban black male subculture—that mystique, rawness, and hipness that can be intimidating and threatening to a suburban white guy.

Here's one example of how that plays out. In a color-blind and racially equal world, we would be judging each other on actions and character, and not on skin color. My initial sense was that, if that were the case, I would not have the need to identify someone as white or black. However, within my first few days in the South, I routinely heard both races describing a person by their skin color. It was in the same context as describing their hair color, gender, or height. When skin color was used in that way, as nothing more than a physical descriptor, maybe that is even more color-blind than carefully avoiding the use of it. It is put on an equal footing with any other external descriptor; nothing more, nothing less. That is what I observed happening while I was in Gulfport, and it eased my apprehension. A bountiful supply of memorable lessons and experiences filled these two weeks, one of the most important being the opportunity to meet and establish meaningful relationships with black people.

The most rewarding news of the day came when I talked with Anna by cell phone about her decision of whether or not to relocate to Fort Collins. She said that she had visited with her friends about it the evening before, and that they had said, "You'd be crazy if you don't." She was extremely excited—with some anxiety too, I would think—about starting a new life in Fort Collins. Anna ended up staying at the Skate Park shelter this night and was planning on starting the cross-country drive the next morning, after completing some final business in Gulfport. We talked more about what Colorado and Fort Collins were like, ideas for job prospects, and I loaned her a road atlas to take with her. Through a friend, Lisa had located a Fort Collins woman by the name of Chris, who was willing to share her house with Anna rent-free for several months. Anna and Lisa talked on the phone, and later in the day, Anna and Chris talked. I also had a combination of excitement and anxiety, the former over being part of this life-changing encounter and the latter about the possibility that it might not work out for some reason.

In sharp contrast to that encouraging development, one of my lowest points while in Gulfport also happened on this day when several clients complained that the donated Monopoly game was without dice. One couple was raging at me that their son had spent about ten minutes setting up the game, and now he was suffering the tragedy of no dice. They demanded that I find them some dice. At that point, all of my frustration and anger with some of our clients' attitudes of entitlement boiled up. Did they not understand that the Red Cross was not the government, that literally tens of thousands of people were volunteering, many using up their vacation time and leaving their families to help them? Some of us were working 17-hour days, much of it spent serving them food and cleaning up the trash that they left on the floors, while they listened to music or watched their portable television. I blurted out something about their finding dice themselves, and left before I spoke words that I would regret. Going into the manager's office to regain my cool I ended up venting some more with George and Dawn. They were very understanding and supportive of my sentiment. We talked about it for a few minutes, then went back to our work.

As it turned out, we registered an additional 16 clients on this day, with one of them being a middle-aged black woman by the name of Cornelia. The words on the black t-shirt that she was wearing were *Love Heals*, a refreshing change from the commercial, inane, or profane words typically seen on t-shirts. I visited with her awhile and saw that she was very traumatized by her hurricane experience. She was barely able to escape the rising storm surge, and several older people in her neighborhood had perished. Although the rest of her family wanted to stay in Gulfport, Cornelia had had enough of living with the threat of hurricanes. She was intending to move to Dallas. She needed first to acquire her $360 check from the Red Cross so that she could afford to move.

Inside the Skate Park shelter

One strangely touching event on this Sunday involved my seeing one of our clients, Al, meticulously separating individual pages of a water-logged, 100-page manuscript, and placing them page by page on several rows of bleachers in the Skate Park building so that they would dry. He had been carrying the pages in a plastic bag since the hurricane and was now attempting to salvage them. Intrigued by the scene, I came over to chat with him. The pages had clearly been typewritten, as opposed to word-processed and printed. I asked him about the subject of the writing and braced myself for something out of the norm. From Al having been with us for several days, I had the impression that he was a very intelligent man, but with some mental health issues. He was a quiet and serious middle-aged man, identifiable in that he always wore glasses with flip-up sun shades. "Well, it's non-fiction," Al answered, "It's basically an existential analysis of environmental conditions observed while I traveled in the Western U.S." Well, now I was *really* curious, and asked if he would mind if I read some of it to get a feel for his topic. "Yea," he responded, although without enthusiasm.

Al's writing was one of the more peculiar assemblages of words that I have ever laid my eyes on. He had a strong vocabulary, with liberal use of multi-syllabic, academic terms. I understood the meaning of each word, and, for the most part, each phrase of words. However, less than half of the time did I understand what he was trying to say with a whole sentence, and never for an entire paragraph. It was as if the hurricane had scattered all of the word phrases and sentences, and jumbled them into an incoherent order. A lot of it had to do with his descriptions of physical landscapes, weather events, and experiences in the Western landscape, but the manuscript bounced around wildly from one point in time and place to another point in time and place. I struggled with what to say to Al, and ended up telling him that I could imagine how important the document was to him, and I complimented him on his tenacity in drying it out.

Later, I was out in the front parking lot, which was the informal "front porch" for our clients to hang out in and have a smoke, and a woman drove up and motioned to me to come over. I noticed the car had a Louisiana license plate. She rolled down the window and said, "Me and my two chillun here are from Nawlins (It took a second for me to recognize this pronunciation as New Orleans). We're headed to Florida to live, but I'm hoping I can get our Red Cross money now 'cause we need it to buy gas. Can I get the money from you?" Before I could answer she gasped loudly, yelled "Look out!" and frantically motioned at something behind me. I turned around to see a van backing up quickly towards us, abruptly stopping no more than three feet from me. The driver had been talking on a cell phone and had not noticed when the woman had pulled up behind him.

It was very fortunate that he happened to notice the end of her car in his rearview mirror, as I didn't have time to jump out of the way and I would have been crushed between the cars. If this close call had occurred during my normal life, it would have been the most adrenaline-evoking moment of my day and it would be very memorable. In this context of multiple days of fast pace, hyper-stimulation and drama, I didn't even think about how close I came to being seriously injured until I read my notes while writing this book after returning home.

As I finished up that conversation, there was some noise out on the street that caught my attention. I looked up and saw Julio waving to me as he pulled over to the curb. Julio had occasionally dropped by the school shelter for some social contact, in particular with Donna, our Spanish-speaking staff member. Julio was originally from the Dominican Republic. His shelter was a nearby tenement building—which probably was not officially habitable—with several other folks. I guessed him to be in his mid-to late-30's, but he later told me he was 45. I had found him to be very friendly and considerate. Walking over to greet him, I could see that he was very upset. He was driving a small rental truck and pulling a trailer with his car loaded on it. From my last conversation with Julio, I knew that he was a house painter, and that he was intending to start a new life in Florida—where he has relatives—after suffering major losses in the hurricane. His last comment to me had been, "I need to get some fresh air in my soul." With much exasperation and inflection in his voice, Julio proceeded to tell me of his unfortunate experiences trying to move. "I was driving to the rental truck agency this morning, all excited about moving to Florida. It was feeling like things were finally getting better and I was leaving my problems and sadness behind. Then, before I was even out of town, my car starting making horrible noises. I didn't want to take a chance on making it worse so I parked it on the shoulder and hitch-hiked a ride to the truck rental place. I drove the truck back to my car and had to load my car on the tow dolly by myself. After driving the truck for only a few miles I could tell something was wrong with how I loaded the car on the dolly. I pulled over to see what had happened. And look at what I did!" Julio pointed to his car and the dolly in disgust. It was apparent that he had loaded the car too far forward on the dolly, severely damaging both front tires and possibly the frame. The car was riding too low and was probably being damaged further by his continuing to pull it. Julio went on by saying, "Now I need to find a tow truck to lift the car off of the dolly and set it back down the right way. I'm too upset to even deal with it now. I'm going to my friend's house and getting some sleep." He loudly complained about his bad luck, climbed back in the truck, and drove off. As he did so, I thought about how much I would relish being a person wealthy enough to hand out money—enough to resolve the problem—to people like Julio. He was hard-working and doing everything to get his life back on track but was having some really bad luck. The next day I tried to reach him at a cell phone number that he had given me, but there was no answer.

Daily shower and Porta-Toilet report: as promised, the Navy Seabee soldiers did come back. They unloaded materials for constructing the showers, but they left before starting construction. "We'll be back tomorrow to build your showers," they promised. This news was disappointing, given that we were expecting 80 or more additional clients in the next day or two. It was even more distressing to think of 100 to 120 people in this facility with only four toilets. We were hoping to have the Porta-Toilets soon.

Because George and more staff members had arrived on this day, I needed to give up my single accommodations in one of the small changing rooms. Ending up in a room with George made sense, because any other staff members would just need to come to one room if any urgent issues developed during the middle of the night. We both turned in shortly after 11:00 p.m., and I was able to fall asleep almost immediately. At some point in the night, I was awakened by what sounded like pressure relief from a steam engine, at about ten-second intervals. Through my grogginess, I gradually realized that it was not a steam engine, nor a dream of a steam engine, but rather George doing some creative snoring. As I dozed in and out over the next hour or two, George added a few more noises to his repertoire. One snore sounded like a sputtering chain saw; another reminded me of the sound of one of those saliva and rinse-water sucking tools used by a dental hygienist. The entertainment value didn't last long, however, so I set up a cot in a secluded corner in the highest portion of the bleachers. That remained my sleeping area for the rest of my time in the Skate Park. I was glad that George took it well when I explained the reason for my relocating. He said that even his lady friend and her cat are not able to sleep in the same room with him.

My sleeping location in the bleachers at the Skate Park shelter

## *Monday, September 19*

*The 15ᵗʰ installment of a Gulfport SunHerald series entitled, "Portraits of Katrina," featured Ashley Grant of Gulfport. Despite losing a car and her home to seven feet of water, Grant was encouraged by friends to move forward with her pre-Katrina plans to fulfill her dream of opening Ashley Grant Fine Furnishings and Resort Interiors. "I feel very proud that I can be a part of helping rebuild a community that I love," said Grant. "I want us all to help rebuild our community. The easiest thing to do is to run as far away as you can."*

*The National Hurricane Center in Miami reported that tropical storm Rita, near the Bahamas with sustained winds of 40 miles per hour, was headed west into the Straits of Florida, and was expected to be in the Gulf, possibly as a hurricane, early this week. The mere thought of that had some displaced New Orleanians skittish yesterday. Once blasé about hurricanes, many are now on edge, concerned even about heavy rainfall. City officials have warned that a 3-inch downpour would be enough to create problems for levees still being repaired. Mayor Ray Nagin suspended his plan to start bringing residents back to the city after hearing the forecast. Much of the city still remains without drinkable water, electric power, and emergency services.*

*In a Monday night National Football League game between the New Orleans Saints and the New York Giants, played in New Jersey, much of the attention was on the relief efforts on the Gulf Coast. Green Bay Packers quarterback and Mississippi coast native Brett Favre was interviewed at half-time. "This is something that is not going away anytime soon," Favre said. "We've got to keep this in the public eye."*

With only a few days remaining before I was to leave Gulfport, my desire to take full advantage of my opportunity to assist people was reaching a fever pitch. Before going to sleep at night, I would ponder additional contacts that I might be able to make and then follow up on them the next day. During the previous night, I had been considering the local immediate need for large sums of money that would complement what FEMA and the Red Cross were doing. I was aware that some very successful fundraising was going on in Fort Collins, through the generosity of the community and an incredibly compassionate offer by the local Bohemian Foundation to match every dollar, one for one, with no limit. Close to two million dollars had been raised, a very impressive amount when you realize that this money was from a surrounding population of only about 200,000 people, equating to an average of $10 for every man, woman, and child. Furthermore, that figure was on top of an additional several million dollars in hurricane relief donations to the Red Cross, Salvation Army, and other non-profits. I decided to contact the Bohemian Foundation to find out how they were distributing those funds and to see if there might be some interest in channeling some of it towards Gulfport.

With Fort Collins being in the one-hour-earlier Mountain Time Zone, I started making phone calls at 9:00 a.m. I was told by the Executive Director of the Bohemian Foundation that the distribution of those funds was being managed by the United Way of Fort Collins and the Community Foundation of Northern Colorado. Fortunately, I was immediately able to reach Ray Caraway, Executive Director of the Community Foundation. "You're calling at just the right time, Jim. We've spent the last few weeks focused on finding the appropriate relief projects and agencies in Louisiana, and now we want to shift our attention to the Mississippi coast," Ray explained. Coincidentally, Ray had previously lived in Louisiana so he had many contacts in that state, but he was much less familiar with Mississippi. "We need to locate the names and numbers of grass-roots non-profit agencies and groups that could disburse our funding quickly, appropriately, and with accountability. The more the donations can go towards a specific, concrete project, the better. With all the damage to these agencies' buildings and their land lines down, it's pretty hard for us sitting up here in Colorado to locate them. If you could help us out with that groundwork, it would be fantastic," Ray told me.

That information was all the encouragement I needed. I started calling immediately, using a local phone book and two cell phones. Over the next few days, through many dozens of phone calls (including one to the Gulfport mayor at 7:00 p.m.), voice messages back and forth, and several trips in George's vehicle to determine if the building of a particular agency was still standing, I was able to secure five viable options for distributing the funds in the Gulfport and Biloxi area: two local United Ways, two local foundations, and one church. I gave these agencies Ray's contact information and vice versa. This arrangement had the real potential to have some huge and positive impacts, so I was hoping fervently that it would work out.

Although we didn't have the rapid influx of clients that had been rumored, this day we did receive another 30 or 35 people, bringing us up to a total of about 65. This day's folks were primarily from the Orange Grove Elementary School that closed as a shelter. It helped that some of the staff from that shelter had now joined us, as there was familiarity between these two respective portions of our new staff and new clients.

One of the new clients not from Orange Grove was Daniel. Another Red Cross volunteer, Steve, had brought him in. Steve told me that the day before Katrina struck, Daniel had evacuated to the Atlanta area by hitch-hiking. Daniel was returning to Gulfport when Steve had come across him and offered to drive him back to his home to survey the damage. As they got closer to Daniel's home, the damage seen out their car windows escalated rapidly. When they were still a block or two from his home, with most of the buildings reduced to debris piles or completely washed from their foundations, Daniel told Steve with tears in his eyes, "Stop. I can't do this." They had turned around and come straight from there to our shelter.

We registered Daniel and walked him to a cot in a location of his choosing. While Steve continued to talk with him, I got some food for him and mentioned Daniel's situation to Brian, a mental health worker. Brian said that he would check in with Daniel soon. As I walked away, I thought about the fact that I had, over the previous week, heard maybe 30 tragic stories related to the hurricane. Extrapolating, I suspected that those stories were probably representative of the 120 or so people that we had as clients. No, there's more to it than that, I thought. Those 30 stories represent what literally *thousands* of people have been through in Mississippi, Louisiana, and Alabama. A sobering and despairing thought, indeed.

During my time with the Red Cross in Gulfport, I was extremely impressed with the mental health workers that I met, especially Brian and Ann. They were very caring and skilled, and I probably referred them to an average of three or four people a day. I have always admired counselors who can empathetically support and provide guidance to clients without being completely overwhelmed with the sadness and despair of the stories and situations they learn about. Such counselors must have the ability to focus on the positive changes and growth that they catalyze rather than on the pain and suffering that they have no control over—which isn't a bad approach to life in general, come to think of it.

This day I contemplated the fact that over the past ten days I had been called "Honey," "Baby," and "Sweetie" at least twice the number of times than in my entire previous life. Many of these terms were used by complete—or nearly so—strangers. Sometimes it was by white women, mostly by black women. (Never by men, I might add.) Much has been written and spoken over the last decades about the homogenization of the American language—that we're losing much of our regional dialects due to the influence of nationwide media, more common travel, and other factors. Although that fact is no doubt true, very discernible differences in the dialects of many regions of the U.S. still exist, and I certainly hope we never lose them. Local dialects add immensely to the pleasure of travel. I would have thought that I was less prone than the average person to assimilating regionalisms in language, but during this afternoon, after a mere one and one-half weeks of influence, I caught myself saying "ya'll" to a few of the clients.

I have noticed that when I am traveling, my ability to overhear other people's remarks is much more acute than when I'm at home. Perhaps it is because I am in adventure mode, with all of my senses more actively engaged and less blocked by running on auto-pilot. It may also be that the dialects and accents of other regions of the U.S. and most certainly of other countries is more attention-get-ting than the language that I am typically exposed to. Regardless of the reasons, I find language to be an enriching and revealing component of travel. On this day, I overheard a despairing remark from one client to another in the bathroom. I might not have paid attention to if it had not been in this setting, and if it had not been said in a southern black dialect: "Hurricanes destroy everything, man—the land, your mind, and your spirit."

Also during the afternoon, I had a chance to visit again with Otis. We talked more about music, and somehow we got off on the topic of his older cousin in Baltimore, who was dying from cancer. Otis said that he felt that he really needed to go there to help take care of her, although he knew it would be hard. A short time later, while talking with her on a cell phone he handed the phone to me. He wanted me to talk with her, for what reason I wasn't sure at the moment. Right from the start, she was crying loudly, telling me that she was very sick and needed to have Otis there to help her. I wasn't sure what to say, other than that I would try to help. After hanging up, Otis apologized for his cousin's crying, saying that she wasn't doing so when he was talking to her. He had previously talked about wanting to go to Baltimore and even had the possibility of gaining a free flight from a private pilots' organization, but he seemed afraid to fly. Within a few hours, I was able to find out the schedule and cost for a bus from Biloxi to Balti-more. It would be $117. I decided that I would help Otis to travel there, if he wanted to go and he needed the money. I talked with him about his desire to go, and he counted up all of the money to his name—$80—which was in his bill-fold. I had a very brief thought of being scammed, and that he had set me up with the woman crying on the phone. I concluded that she was an extremely good actress, if that were the case, and that Otis had not seemed dishonest. I rationalized that there was only a small chance of Otis not using the money for the intended purpose, and that it was definitely worth the risk, so I handed him $60. He expressed moderate appreciation and told me that he would leave on Wednesday evening.

As part of setting up the shelter the previous Saturday, I had written up a list of our shelter rules on a poster board and placed it near the registration desk in the front so that everyone could see it. About 15 rules were included, most of them common courtesy sorts of things like respecting other people's property, cleaning up after yourself, no smoking inside, and keeping quiet between 10:00 p.m. and 7:00 a.m. Regardless of this list being posted, however, we were gradually losing control of the clients' behavior. We had one officer from the Harrison County Sheriff's Department with us around the clock since we opened, but we would be transitioning to a private security firm this coming weekend. One of the county officers warned us that we had better get the situation under control soon, while they were still there, because the private security people would probably not be very effective.

For example, one of our female clients reported to me that a male client had inappropriately brushed up against her and that he had also done the same thing to a female friend of hers. We located the man's name, looked it up on the county's list of registered sex offenders, and found that he wasn't included. Of course, that fact only meant that he hadn't registered as a sex offender in that county and it didn't rule out the possibility of his having committed sex offenses elsewhere. Our deputy on staff informed the women that they could either charge him, in which case he would be taken to jail, or they could just leave it as a complaint with the shelter, in which case he would be evicted. They chose the latter and the deputy told him of the accusations. He did not deny it and he was ordered to pick up his stuff and leave, which he did.

To help supplement the poorly-working air conditioning, two huge, commercial-sized fans were positioned on the floor of the rink, operating continuously. We had been having a slight but increasing problem with clients occasionally moving the direction of a fan so that they could benefit from the moving air. This afternoon, one of our white male clients, probably in his late 50's, had become annoyed at some younger black men who had moved the fan. In complaining to me, he had described the men by using the extremely offensive "N word" as a racial slur. I was completely shocked and immediately looked around to see who might have heard him. I was relieved to see that no one else was nearby, especially a black person, not as much out of concern that it probably would have started a fight, but more out of concern for not wanting someone to be emotionally hit by his crude remark. Livid with him, I said, "We realize that we need to do something about the fans but that doesn't excuse your language. If you use that word one more time you'll be thrown out." He showed little emotion, turned, and walked away.

Later in the day, two instances of kindness occurred that helped ease the sting of the racial insult and tension. A white man came into the shelter, toting a greeting card the size of a poster board. He explained that it was from children in Tennessee who had raised money for the Red Cross by holding a car wash fundraiser. He lived in Gulfport, and his wife's relatives lived in the Tennessee town. The greeting card had all of the kids' handprints on it in bright colors of tempura paint. The message expressed that the hurricane victims were in their thoughts and prayers. We posted it on the wall near the entrance for all to see and appreciate.

Greeting poster from Tennessee children

The second instance of kindness occurred when a white client initiated a routine with the children in the shelter, in which he sat in a chair out in the middle of the rink and created all sorts of balloon hats and animals. The kids squealed with delight and ran back to show their families.

Daily shower and Porta-Toilet report: on the shower front, we took a step backwards on this day, as the Navy Seabees came by and loaded up the shower-making materials and then left. Presumably, they were taking them to another site for easier assembly, and then returning with them, but we had no idea when. The toilet situation reached its most dire point this morning when the water pressure became so low that only one of the four toilets was flushing. Fortunately, the problem was resolved within a few hours. Even better news came with the arrival of ten Porta-Toilets, now nicely lined up in the parking lot.

Although it's hard to complain when you have a volunteer organization preparing and delivering meals, the timing of deliveries left a little bit to be desired on this day. Our lunch arrived a bit late at 1:00 p.m. and the dinner arrived very early at 3:00 p.m. We ended up holding the dinner food in the insulated Cambro containers as long as we thought safe, then still had an early dinner.

I was able to get away for a 40-minute run in the afternoon, which included viewing another portion of the most devastated strip along the beach. Even with the advanced development and high quality of news videotape and photographs, catastrophic damage of this sort was so much more dramatic and real when seen firsthand. Whether it's the jump from two dimensions to three dimensions, or from one or two senses to all five senses, the scene registers so much deeper into one's psyche.

Destroyed motel near Gulfport beach

Remnants of Gulfport's beach boardwalk

The most creative and clear-headed time for me is during that dream-like transition from sleep consciousness to wakefulness. I prefer to begin waking early enough to have at least 20 minutes in this state of horizontal reverie before needing to hit the floor and get going with the day. If at all possible, I like to have the benefit of pondering any substantial personal issues or dilemmas in this way before coming to a decision. I suppose it could be called "waking on it," as opposed to "sleeping on it." On occasion, what seems like a brilliant idea during this time period gets relegated to the dim-witted heap when considered under the more discerning light of day. Other times however, my early-morning ideas and tentative decisions do hold up and get implemented. During my time in Gulfport, however, I did not have the luxury of such gradual awakening. I did have a modified, lower quality version of it before going to sleep, given that I usually couldn't fall asleep soon anyway. On this night, my starting point was from the previous day's musings about how rewarding and enjoyable it would be if I were wealthy enough to be able to donate substantial amounts of money to people and agencies. The greatest pleasure would come from making such gifts on-the-spot after an informal and discreet assessment of the need, but without any formality of grant application or waiting period. It would be a sort of "deliberate and specific act of kindness," as opposed to a "random act of kindness."

Rather than wasting any time fantasizing about winning the lottery, I thought about what I could more realistically do to acquire a modest amount of money for this purpose. Up until this point, I had been planning on writing an unpublished journal for the benefit of family, friends, and myself. During this episode of pondering, I concluded that as long as I was going to write a journal it would be worth the additional effort to print or publish it, sell copies of it, and dedicate half of the proceeds to the hurricane relief effort. Of course, there were the small details that I had never written professionally and knew absolutely nothing about getting a book published, but that problem did not seem insurmountable. I entered the world of sleep with the pleasant vision of handing out money to people with urgent needs.

### Tuesday, September 20

*Tropical storm Rita was upgraded to a Category 2 hurricane, as it swept across the Florida Keys with gusts to 102 miles per hour. Hurricane Rita is expected to intensify into a large and dangerous Category 3 or stronger hurricane—one with sustained winds reaching or exceeding 131 miles per hour. The threat of a direct assault on devastated southeast Louisiana, Mississippi and Alabama appears to be easing. However, Texans, including those in the heavily populated Houston/Galveston area, face an escalating risk that Hurricane Rita could grow stronger and crash into that state's vulnerable coastline late Friday or Saturday.*

*The price of ail surged more than $4.00 a barrel, the biggest one-day price jump ever, amid worries that Hurricane Rita could hit U.S. oil facilities in the Gulf of Mexico this week, striking another blow at an industry struggling to recover from Hurricane Katrina.*

After the usual quick breakfast, my morning began with a trip to the Gulfport Red Cross headquarters, which had moved to a new location about five days earlier. The purpose of the trip for me and four others was to do our "out-processing" with the Red Cross. My original plan was to fly out of Montgomery (a four and one-half hour drive away) at 7:00 a.m. on the upcoming Friday, but I decided it would be better to fly out of Mobile (a one-hour drive away) on Thursday. I didn't want to take any chances on a mess-up, so I decided to complete this administrative work on this day.

Red Cross out-processing took about 45 minutes, consisting of checking in at several staffed tables and completing tasks related to the use of Red Cross vehicles, debit card expenditures and arranging for a shuttle, if needed, to travel to an airport. Another stop was at the mental health table where a counselor asked several questions such as "How was the experience for you?" and "How are you feeling?" presumably to ascertain if you were still in one piece, emotionally speaking. Apparently I said the right things to pass the test.

On the way back from the Red Cross headquarters we dropped off one person of our group at the Gulfport Airport, as he was done with his deployment and heading home. Adjacent to this airport was the National Guard facility and runway, and as we drove by it, we happened to notice Air Force One taxiing in. This occasion was the second of President Bush's visits to Gulfport during my two-week stay, and I happened to see the jet both times.

Later in the morning I returned to the Gulfport Airport, this time to take Dawn to her going-home flight. We had the chance to visit a bit more during the 15-minute drive. She talked about some of her past jobs and the places where she had lived, expressing a desire to move again if the right situation came along. Because I was starting to think more about my leaving I was wondering whom of all of the Red Cross staffers and clients that I had met I might cross paths with in the future. It's good to know that at least we staffers had shared all of our contact information so that we could initiate contact if desired. The intensity of the experience more than outweighed the brevity, to the point that the memories of some of these relationships would rival the memories of even my college or high school buddies.

Daniel was considerably more upbeat this day because he had been able to initiate the process with FEMA and had received his $360 from Red Cross. He offered, in a very genuine and caring manner, to help out with work at the shelter, however it was needed. I later saw him assisting with serving one of the meals. Daniel shared with me a story that was very influential to him in the development of his character. "When I was 14 or 15 years old, this girl that I had fallen for gave me the brush-off. I was devastated and moping around. My grandfather sat me down and I don't remember his exact words, but it was something to the effect that, 'You have two choices. You can continue to cry and feel sorry for yourself, or you can pull yourself up and make the most of what you do have,'" Daniel said. It was obvious that Daniel had chosen the second option, given the way he was living his life.

In the afternoon, we found out from a client, and then confirmed it by looking in the local newspaper, that the Red Cross had given out checks the previous day to qualified hurricane victims about one-half mile from our location. This place was the closest distribution point thus far, yet we had not previously heard about it. If it remained at that location and if they could arrive there early enough, our clients might finally receive their checks.

During the evening, I spent some time chatting with clients out in front of the building. We had erected a canopy to help provide some shade and had moved some benches under it from inside one of the changing rooms. I introduced myself to Lamont, a client that I had not previously talked with. His home was in Atlanta, and he was in Gulfport working for a contractor who was hired to lay rolls of concertina razor barbed wire along the south side of the railroad tracks to keep looters out. He was an electrician by trade, but he wasn't able to find that type of work in Atlanta. Lamont was intending to stay down here for at least a month, and he obviously missed his wife and two children. He proudly showed me pictures of them.

Lamont's story spurred my thinking about the local employment situation. I imagined that residents of this region had mixed feelings about out-of-town people coming here for short-term employment. It was probably fine if they were supplementing the resident labor force, but not very welcome if their work was taking a job away from a local person. From what I could observe, it seemed that there was a strong market for workers, especially in the service sector, an indicator of which was the extreme lack of employees in the local Wal-Mart when I was there shopping for supplies. The checkout clerk said they were having a hard time hiring people. I was surprised, because I had heard that all 29 casinos in Gulfport and Biloxi had been destroyed and that they had employed an average of 1,000 people per casino. Furthermore, the vast majority of retail stores and restaurants were still closed. I was quite curious about this economic disconnect.

The weather was a popular topic of conversation during this day. The sweltering heat and high humidity had continued, with a high temperature of 98 degrees outside, and 91 degrees inside the building. It was a bit reassuring to know that I wasn't being a complete wimp in thinking that it was hot, after hearing four or five local folks complain about it. With some climatic irony, I overheard a radio broadcast in which the announcer mentioned the developing drought, as they had not received even a trace of rain in the 20 days since the last of the Katrina-related torrential rains. The weather also had people's attention with the news that a new tropical storm—named Rita—was upgraded to hurricane status and moving on a path similar to Katrina. Some person or agency had donated two televisions, so we used one for clients to watch movies on DVD and the other one for watching news.

On this day we grew to about 80 clients and were still expecting more. We were now at the point that the size of our shelter and our level of staffing was justified.

However, two-thirds of the 12 staff members were scheduled to leave within the next week, so there would have to be some continual re-staffing to offset the attrition.

A new client who had recently been to her destroyed neighborhood in New Orleans registered in the evening. She needed a place to stay for the night while traveling to the home of a family member further down the road. One of our other clients overheard her and came to me saying, "You're not going to allow her to stay in the shelter, are you? She's probably infected with God knows what toxic stuff, and my boy has asthma. I don't want him to be at risk." I wasn't exactly certain of the actual epidemiological risk, but I was pretty certain it was infinitesimal. Still, I tried to be diplomatic and told her that it was only for one night and that the New Orleans woman's cot was on the other side of the rink from her family.

Shower report for the day: not only did we not hear from or see any of the Navy Seabees or our long-promised showers, but another group of three soldiers showed up (from where, I'm not sure) and informed me, "We were instructed to come here to assess your need for showers." They had not the slightest knowledge of the other group of soldiers also building showers, let alone the status of them. We were back to square one with this group. They left muttering something about going back to talk with their sergeant.

### Wednesday, September 21

*The official death toll from Hurricane Katrina passed 1,000, as Hurricane Rita underwent explosive intensification over the bathtub warm waters of the Gulf of Mexico, leaping past infamous Katrina to become the third most intense Atlantic Basin hurricane on record. During this evening its pressure plunged to 897 millibars, besting deadly Katrina's lowest barometric reading by 5 millibars and the pressure was still dropping. The storm is taking aim on the Texas Gulf coast where hurricane watches are posted and mass evacuations are underway in anticipation of an early Saturday morning landfall.*

*The remarkable national outpouring of financial support for Hurricane Katrina relief efforts has resulted in a major impact to local non-profit agencies. Donations to such agencies are significantly down, as donors divert their typical contributions to such groups. In Fort Collins, Crossroads Safehouse is having to dip into its operating funds reserves for the first time in its 25-year history.*

First thing this morning, I decided to go for a run before it got too hot. I decided to combine my run with an investigation of the nearby distribution point for Red

Cross checks. Despite being about 6:15 a.m. and still not completely light, it was already warm and muggy. The air felt very heavy in my lungs. Even if I hadn't known the location, I could have found it by following the traffic. As I got within several hundred yards, I could see the long line of cars, National Guard and police vehicles with their lights on and directing traffic, and a large parking lot filling up with cars. The building was a movie theatre four-plex that had been apparently damaged enough by the hurricane to still be closed, although it had minimal external damage. They were using the parking lot and the adjacent vacant land to conduct the distribution of the checks. Several large canopies were set up for shade, with folding tables and chairs set up underneath, but the Red Cross staff was not yet at the tables. As you would expect, numerous policemen and National Guard were present for security and crowd control.

When I had witnessed the devastation along the coast it literally caused me to gasp with the realization of the power and strength of the hurricane. When I heard tragic stories told with tears streaming down faces, I was struck with the depth of the hurricane's impact. What I experienced in the next few minutes provided a dramatic image of the breadth of the tragedy.

I slowed to a walk as I got closer to the canopies and was shocked when I saw the full extent of the line of people, snaking around the building. A full range of adult ages were represented in the stalled line, with a small sprinkling of children and babies. Shorts and t-shirts were the common dress, with many hats and umbrellas for shelter from the sun. Most were standing, although some were seated on the curb and others were seated on folding chairs that they brought. As might be expected, the mood was subdued and the people appeared tired. There was little conversation among them. A Red Cross volunteer was walking along the line of people with a cart that held bottled water, handing it out freely to whoever desired it.

I walked to the end of the line with two objectives in mind. First, I wondered if any of our shelter's clients were in line. Second, I wanted to estimate the number of people, which I guessed to be about 500. Five hundred people waiting in a line at 6:30 a.m., knowing that they might have to spend another three hours in the sun and the heat for the purpose of receiving $360 per person in the household. Many of them had already spent countless hours trying to reach the toll-free number or driving and walking around town to each rumored new location of the disbursement stations.

Approximately 500 people in line for Red Cross disbursements

That scene was a dramatic illustration of not only the wrath of the hurricane on people's financial conditions but also the impoverished status of many of them to begin with. After returning home, I looked up the U.S. Department of Commerce statistics, and found that the average per capita income in the U.S. is $32,900. The state with the highest per capita income is Connecticut, at $45,400. The state with the lowest per capita income is Mississippi at $24,600.

While starting to walk away from the long line, I happened to strike up a conversation with a Hispanic woman sitting on a curb with a boy. Her husband was holding their place in line. They had used to live in Colorado Springs, where she did office-cleaning and he had worked construction. "We moved here because we heard there was more work. It is easier to find work here, but the benefits aren't good at all," she said, while tending to her son. For the umpteenth time, I listened to someone tell me about suffering greatly from the forces of nature. "We can count our blessings, though. Some good friends of ours bought several rooms' worth of new furniture in July, after saving up for it for six years. They lost all of it, with no insurance. Even worse than that, three older folks in our neighborhood drowned. Compared to that, yea, we're doing okay," she said, with a mixture of despair and thankfulness.

When I got back to the Skate Park shelter, I was greeted by a Red Cross volunteer from headquarters who said that she was there to directly assist our clients in obtaining their $360 checks, in particular three of our clients who were deaf. If we had had some advance knowledge of her coming, we could have saved several of our clients the discomfort of waiting several hours in the long line outside in the heat at the theatre parking lot. One of these clients, a heavy-set woman by the name of Cornelia, had actually walked there twice. The first time was at 4:30 a.m., only to be turned back by the police for violating the curfew.

Still, we were happy that that the Red Cross volunteer had arrived to help. About eight of our clients were able to receive their checks from her in relatively easy fashion. I asked her how they prevented fraud from people who suffered no damage or from victims applying multiple times (so-called "frequent flyers"). I assumed that she would have a laptop tied into some national database. She had no such technology, saying there was really no way that she could prevent fraud, and she had to rely on trust. My impression was that she was speaking only for the process that she was undertaking to help out a select group of people in the shelters, rather than the more typical process used for the masses standing in long lines. I hoped that my impression was accurate.

A couple of our Red Cross volunteers enjoyed caring for the children in our shelter. They set up a play area in the corner, complete with a television for videos, some games, and art supplies. For a while the children were drawing pictures, and I was admiring their work. Jacob, the seven-year-old boy with an affinity for fire, showed me one of his drawings. I saw that it was a house with some projections on either side. I couldn't tell what they were, so I asked him. "It's a house with wings, so the family can fly away in it when the next hurricane comes," He proudly explained. A few of the other children's pictures related to the hurricane were a bulldozer demolishing what was left of a house and a bus that was said to be going to rescue people from the New Orleans Super Dome. I was reminded of how my two sons, ages two and five at the time, had processed their emotions and memories about the Spring Creek flood by play-acting as emergency response workers for many months after the event.

Some concern was expressed by a parent who indicated that one of the new male clients was showing an unusual degree of interest in the children. We determined his name and once again checked the registered sex offenders list. He was not listed. Because he had not done anything illegal or directly inappropriate, we just informed the staff of the situation, with the request to keep an eye on him and the children. One of our shelter rules was that one parent was supposed to be with children at all times, but that procedure was clearly not always followed.

During the afternoon, some additional Red Cross folks came by looking for prospective clients interested in being housed on a Carnival Cruise Liner anchored in Mobile, Alabama. They preferred seniors but would consider others as well. Within a few hours, Dennis, Ron, and a family of five excitedly signed up to go. Ron had spent several decades on fishing boats, so no Dramamine would be needed for him. I joked with him that he certainly chose a hard way to gain a ticket to a cruise, going through a hurricane and losing everything. "Well, if I had my druthers I wouldn't take a cruise to Mobile Bay either, but I'm happy with it in this situation!" Ron responded.

Although I had first met John about a week earlier back at the school shelter, I was able to spend some more time visiting with him this day. John was another of the dozen or so clients for whom I will have the most indelible memories. The most noticeable descriptor when I first saw him was the fact that he was in a wheelchair and that he had screws and metal bars attached to both of his lower legs. When I conjure up a mental image of him now, however, I think of his bearded face, his penetrating but soft eyes, the worn-out straw cowboy hat on his head, and most especially, his courage. Previously at the school shelter, he had been trying to locate an occupational therapist who could secure some crutches and help him to re-strengthen his legs so that he could eventually walk again on his own. He had waited out front of our shelter for one and one-half hours in the dripping heat to eventually catch a bus ride to the local hospital. When he arrived, the hospital staff did nothing more than give him the name of a few occupational therapists, information he could have found on his own with a phone book at the shelter.

On this day I benefited by becoming better acquainted with John. To most of his friends, John was known as Cowboy, in reference to his hat and rugged Western-looking face. He told me that he was 43 years old, but I would have guessed 50. To say that Cowboy had had a challenging five months is the ultimate understatement. With some sadness in his voice, but no bitterness, he reeled off the chronology of his misfortunes. "About five months ago my woman-friend died. That was tough to deal with. She was real important to me, especially since I don't really have any family any more. Both of my parents died quite awhile ago, and I'm not in contact much with my brother and sister. Then, four months ago, I was working construction and fell off of a 20-foot roof. It shattered both of my lower legs, and was the worst pain I've ever had. I didn't lose consciousness but it might have been better if I did." I waited while he took a sip of water and gathered his thoughts to continue. "About a month ago when Katrina hit, I was in my first floor apartment lying on my couch. The only way I could get around was in a wheelchair or crawling. The water began coming under my front door and then it broke through a window and began rising inside. It was coming up real fast, so I had to scoot backwards up my stairs. The worst part was that I could smell gasoline. I feared an explosion more than I did drowning." Cowboy ended up surviving, and was now doing his best to resurrect his life. He desperately wanted to be able to walk and work again. Earlier that day, a volunteer had helped Cowboy take a "shower," using a garden hose connected to an outside faucet. It was the first time in three and one-half weeks that he was able to get fully clean. His previous washings had been limited to whatever he could do himself with a washcloth. Cowboy was also very pleased that he was able finally to gain his $360 from Red Cross. Because of the shower and $360, Cowboy told me with a smile on his face, "Everything's going good. I'm still blessed."

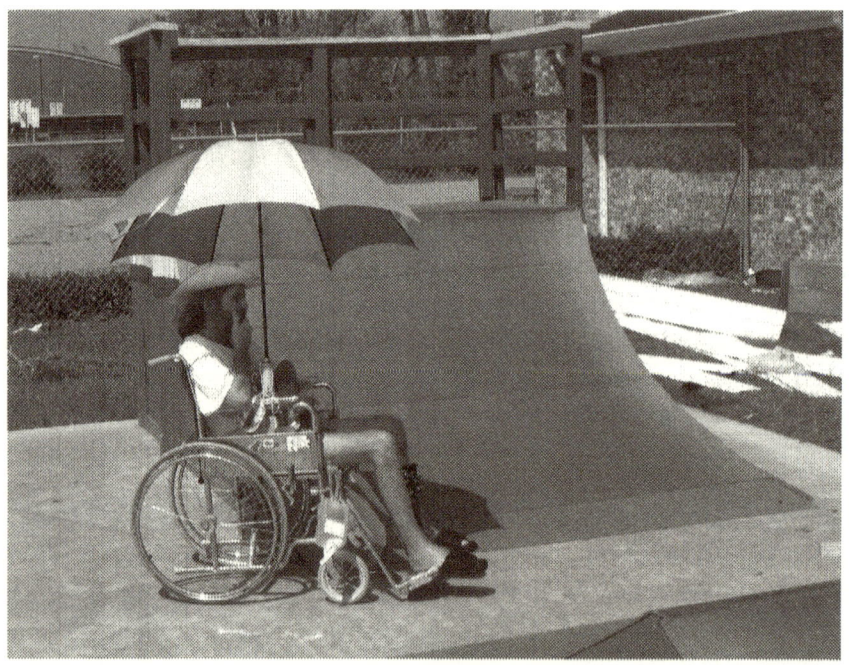

"Cowboy" at Skate Park shelter

In the early evening, we had a period of panic when Amy, the mother of Wilson, the eleven-year-old boy, noticed that she had not seen him for a while. "Why don't I start looking for him while you finish your dinner," I offered. Not finding him inside the building, I checked outside in the area where he had been previously playing. Wilson was nowhere to be seen. I became moderately concerned, so I recruited three or four Red Cross staffers to help me look. At about this time Amy joined our search, and I was taken aback that she didn't seem to be nearly as concerned as me (although that could relate to the fact that this was her ninth child, and she had undoubtedly been through similar situations that had turned out fine). We continued to search for another ten minutes, enlisting the deputy to help us, before finally finding him hiding in the rink area. Amy calmly asked him to keep her posted on his whereabouts, and that was the end of it.

In the late evening, I was informed by Drew, a Red Cross volunteer, that there was an older client who was not able to make it to the bathroom in time, and that he did not have any more clothes. Drew and another volunteer went to the nearby Wal-Mart to purchase some clothes for him. By this time of night, the Wal-Mart was closed to the public, but they were staying open "24/7" for any Red Cross customers, definitely a great service.

At about the same time one of our clients with some chronic health problems became noticeably worse. We knew that she had been depressed, having already been to the hospital once for her diabetes and related problems. We received a phone call from the Red Cross national headquarters with the news that the client's sister had been talking with her, and that the client had indirectly threatened suicide. We knew that she had more than enough prescription drugs to cause herself serious injury or death if she desired. Over the course of the next two or three hours many steps of assessing her condition were taken, with the involvement of nurses, our two deputies providing security, a Red Cross mental health worker, and two E.M.T.'s. We were not able to force her to go to the hospital against her will, because none of us had directly observed or heard any suicide threat. Furthermore, she responded that she did not want to hurt herself (even though she thought a long time before answering the question). We were able to convince her to turn over her medications, although we weren't certain that we had all of them. Fortunately, her cot was in a location that was easily observed, so we had all of our night staffers keep a very close eye on her until morning. She awoke the next morning feeling better but still a cause for concern.

A highlight of the day was discovering about 20 notes handwritten by elementary school children from Maryland on cards that another staff member had posted on the glass wall of the rink. The husband of the school's counselor had apparently volunteered with the Red Cross, working somewhere in the Gulfport area. The most touching one that I read said, in crayon, "Don't Give up Hope!" on the outside. On the inside, the following was written:

---

*Dear Hurricane victims,*

*Even though you may have been going through a tough time, don't give up hope. I hope that soon you will have a place to live and all of this will be over. But remember there are people all over trying their best to help you through this time.*

*Sincerely,*

*Jessica*

I copied down the name and address of the school counselor so that I could later contact her with an expression of gratitude for their children's kind deed.

Last shower report: after yet another day of no action by the military or anyone else in obtaining or building portable showers, two clients and a staff person decided to take matters into their own hands. They purchased the necessary supplies, primarily lumber and a tarp, to build a shower outside, using an exterior faucet and a garden hose to provide the water. Although the water was unheated, in this part of the country and at this time of the year it was still relatively warm, not to mention that the outside air temperatures were in the 80's and 90's. This crude but effective shower was an extremely popular improvement to our shelter.

An older couple showed up during the evening with the initial desire to sleep in their car in the shelter parking lot. In talking with them, we learned that they had had a bad experience at the Good Deeds shelter, leaving there out of fear. According to their report, they had walked out of the shelter towards their car to discover that there was a gang of teenagers breaking into it. The man working security was unwilling to confront the gang. As a result, they didn't want to leave their car and belongings unattended here, nor did they feel safe when they looked inside our shelter. We eventually convinced them that it would be more comfortable and safe inside, where people's activities could be watched more closely.

On the way to Wal-Mart to buy some supplies, we drove Otis, the client I had given money to, to a nearby location, where he met a friend of his who was going to drive him to Mobile. From there he would be taking a bus to Baltimore to be with his cousin. We shook hands and I told him to drop a line or visit me sometime in Colorado, but I doubted that it would ever happen. I'll never forget him.

### Thursday, September 22

*With massive and powerful Hurricane Rita bearing down on the Texas and Louisiana coast, an estimated 2.5 million people heeded calls for evacuation and jammed the road-ways in sweltering heat, causing a 100-mile backup. The crisis was almost the reverse of the Katrina disaster, which trapped people in their homes or public buildings. Travelers became trapped in the traffic, running out of gas, watching their engines boil over, getting little information on the radio about alternative routes, and sometimes choosing to return home rather than continuing. The scene had people around the country wondering whether their cities, or any modern metropolis, could handle the evacuation challenge in a natural or man-made disaster.*

*An editorial in the Boston Globe reported the stunning role reversal of the United States accepting Hurricane Katrina relief from some of the world's poorest nations. "The switch may be a bit embarrassing for official Washington but it is good for the hearts of the U.S. citizenry and throughout the global neighborhood," wrote the editorial board. Bangladesh gave $1 million to the relief effort, the equivalent of $65 million in the currency of that country, where the average wage translates into $450 a year. "We hear the common cry of humanity," said a press aide at the Bangladesh Embassy in Washington. Ethiopia donated $100,000 to the Bush-Clinton Katrina Fund. Their Embassy spokesperson stated, "It is a gesture, a sign of solidarity, and expresses our condolences to America and its people."*

I awoke on my last day with conflicting emotions. I had never been away from my wife and children for this long, and I was elated at the prospect of returning to be with them by the end of the day. They bring the most meaning and grounding to my life, and I missed them greatly. However, there was another feeling that was hard to pinpoint—something like sorrow, but I wasn't sure over what. It was not the sadness and grief that I was feeling for all of the loss and pain that I had witnessed. By now I knew that feeling well and this one was not the same. After mulling it over, I realized that it was sadness and disappointment over the prospect of losing such a rich and deep connection with other people's lives. Granted, I understood that it is not within my personal make-up to do this kind of emotionally intense work for very long, and I would not choose to do so. Still, I had discovered that there was a very addictive quality to what I had experienced, not so much to the adrenaline factor of being in crisis mode, but more from the profound gratification at making a big difference in others' lives when they are most in need of support. Part of me didn't want to leave an environment in which I could so easily accomplish that end. As I packed up my belongings, I suddenly realized that my strong sentiments about helping people in critical situations and connecting with them on a deeper emotional and spiritual level was a major element of the meaning and purpose for which I had been searching.

Although much of my life experience had centered on directly or indirectly serving people, the vast majority of it had been providing relatively privileged services to fairly well-off people. From the reference point of Psychology 101 and Maslow's Hierarchy of Needs, my work has focused much more on the middle/higher needs of aesthetics and education. What I found so stimulating about working at the shelters, in terms of Maslow's Hierarchy, was that it mixed the lowest, most basic human needs of food and shelter with the very highest levels of what Maslow referred to as transcendence and self actualization, and what I would simply term spiritual. The instances in which I felt that I was touching the spiritual level occurred mainly when I was conversing with hurricane victims who were processing their experience in a meaningful, sacred and/or religious context. Curiously, at brief times I also felt that sense of holiness—even worship—when serving food or setting up cots for our clients. It was as if my actions of helping others at the most basic level of need elevated the experience to the highest level of existence. Doing so gave me a glimpse of an understanding of how Mother Teresa could have lived such a holy and spirit-filled life by completely dedicating herself to providing the most elemental of physiological needs to some of the most destitute people on the planet.

Because of the dynamic nature of the shelter, any one staff person or client leaving hardly created a stir. Over the course of a week, 50 new clients might register and 50 others move out. During the same week, we could have five or more Red Cross volunteers end their deployment and another five or so start anew. There was also the continual background bedlam of people coming and going, and the miscellaneous activities, interactions, and crises. So, my leaving was a non-event. It seemed that most of the people I had grown closest to, whether Red Cross staffers or clients, had already left. To those remaining I said my goodbyes, and then I walked out the door and was on my way home. I loaded up my gear in a Red Cross vehicle with George at the wheel. He needed to meet with some Red Cross folks and had obligingly offered to take me to the Gulfport headquarters where I would board the Red Cross shuttle to the Mobile airport.

At the headquarters, I could see Red Cross volunteers who had just arrived and also those who were ending their two-or three-week deployments. The differences between the two groups were evident. The fresh volunteers acted very excited and talkative within their groups, looking around and taking in the new environment. The clothes they wore seemed to have been just laundered and ironed. In contrast, the volunteers shipping out were clearly more subdued, fatigued, and wrinkled, with a lost-in-thought look about them.

George and I shook hands, and I thanked him for the very complimentary evaluation that he had written for me. I wished him well during his remaining week and promised that I would be in touch.

The relative quiet, comfort and normalcy of the next six or seven hours of shuttle drive, waiting in the Mobile and Atlanta airports, and the two flights home offered time to decompress and reflect a bit about my experience. Many of my thoughts were about the many people whom I had met. Going through such an intense and roughhewn experience with others can be truly bonding, at least with the ones with whom there is a kindred connection. For at least five of the Red Cross staff, I felt close enough that I was certain I would maintain contact. My emotional connection to a handful of the hurricane victims ran deeper though, probably in direct relation to the more profound level of their experience and their sharing. I thought of Trent, Mary, Vinh, Anna, Cowboy, Otis, Julio, and Clare. I would be seeing Anna again in Fort Collins, and I silently prayed for her well-being in her travel. Since the abrupt closure of the school shelter had sent us in different directions, I regretted not feeling closure with Clare. I was curious about how she was doing, as I was with all of the others. Although I fully intended to make an effort to contact many of them by phone or mail in the coming months, I had a hunch that I wouldn't be able to reach many of them. What I did absolutely know was that these people would forever remain in my memory as inspirations, each in a different way. They had all exhibited courage and strong character and were working on making the most out of their tragic experiences.

Just as we reached our cruising altitude out of Atlanta, the pilot directed the passengers to look out the windows to the south. On the horizon were large cumulonimbus clouds, thunderheads that were part of the outer rings of Hurricane Rita, whose eye was at least 200 miles away in the Gulf of Mexico. With the imminent landfall of another major hurricane on the Gulf coast less than two days away, it seemed that in a superficial way, my journey had come full circle. From a more personal perspective, though, it would be better described as one turn of a spiral, because I knew that I had grown from the experience and that I was a very different person from whom I had been two weeks earlier. I knew, though, that it would take much more contemplation and writing to figure out exactly in what ways.

# 6

# *Back Home*

o o o o o o o o o o o o o o o o o o o o o o o o o o o o o o o o

*Too often we underestimate the power of a touch, a smile, a kind word, a listening ear, an honest compliment, or the smallest act of caring, all of which have the potential to turn a life around.*

—*Leo Buscaglia*

If you're at all like me, you'll know that there is inevitably a difficult re-entry phase in transitioning back to the real world after returning from a vacation, an adventurous travel, or a spiritual journey. Regardless of the type of experience and its rewards—pleasure and relaxation, excitement and adrenaline, education and intellectual stimulation, or personal growth and spiritual insight—the challenge is to maintain the benefit as long as possible, integrate it into the routine of your normal life, and draw nourishment from it until the next occasion.

My Red Cross experience was so unique and I felt such emotional impact that upon my return I couldn't really define what I had been through, let alone how I would integrate it in my life. What I did know was that it had been very profound in a deeply personal and spiritual way. I was in the grasp of some sort of transformation, with my only point of reference being my recollection of an experience at the age of 18. I had thought of that experience as a metanoia, meaning a spiritual change of mind and heart, and this felt similar. God was no longer an abstract, theosophical concept, because a divine presence had touched my soul. There was grist for spiritual insight and a renewed sense of purpose in my life, but it still needed much pondering, refinement, and coalescing. In sharp contrast to my typical feeling of slight melancholy when returning from an adventurous trip or meaningful experience, this time I felt energized and excited, as if the adventure was really just beginning.

After my return, I relished my time back with family and friends, and I re-engaged myself with work and home responsibilities, but most of my emotional and cognitive presence—for at least a month—was still in Mississippi. As an indicator of the depth of the impact to my psyche, I had extremely vivid and emotional dreams and nightmares for ten straight nights after returning. Typically, I do not recall my dreams upon waking, and I did not remember any dreams while I was in Mississippi. After I came back, though, it was as if the radical change to a relatively placid life during my waking hours was too much for my sub-conscious to handle, so it created its own bizarre assemblage of hurricane and shelter-centered plot lines at night. In at least two of these dreams/nightmares, I was fighting for my life against the raging wind and water of a hurricane. Several mornings I awoke thinking that I was still at a Gulfport shelter, with the thought only dissipating after opening my eyes and realizing I was home.

That such an experience would result in a remarkable change is not surprising. After all, it would be hard to design a more ideal spiritual boot camp environment, where the participant is physically and emotionally broken down as a set-up for being thrown life-lines of new beliefs or values. Ten straight days of physically-exhausting, 17-hour work days and sleep deprivation in a surreal environment, while being bombarded with dozens of desperate people venting frustration, anger, despair, and grief, as well as the demonstrations of extreme courage and compassion and the opportunity to connect with and assist people in a very intimate and spiritual way. All these experiences create a pretty good recipe for a conversion of some sort.

Now, lest you gain the wrong impression that my work days were the norm for a Red Cross shelter worker, I should acknowledge that the excessive length and intensity was largely of my own choosing. It was not a masochistic urge or a desire for some version of glory but simply what seemed right for me to do in that situation with the opportunities presented. Twelve-hour work days and a significantly less manic approach were more the standard procedure with equally effective results in the long run, I suspect. Also, I think that my experience was intensified by the fact that I came into it predisposed for a transformation, given the pretext of the spiritual search that I was in the midst of.

In this spiritual boot camp, there was no pre-determined plan by any person or group to either program or de-program me. As I perceive it, the life lines that were thrown to me were the result of my soul being receptive to what God was presenting to me. The emotional and spiritual experiences that I had were not the doctrine of any particular religion, however. The lessons and insights that I eventually deciphered strike me as much more fundamental, more universal, in some ways a common chord to many of the world's religions. But I'm getting ahead of myself. The identification and synthesis of these divine messages was a process that took several months after returning. In some cases these pieces of spiritual insight and life direction resulted from cognitive thought and reflection; other times they bubbled up in dreams or a hypnogogic state halfway between sleep and wakefulness. At times they became gradually clear; at other times there was an out-of-the-blue epiphany.

Although I had already made the decision to write a memoir about my experience while at the Skate Park shelter, it did not blossom into a full-blown compulsion until I returned. I felt that to do so would be a natural extension of the same force that had compelled me to volunteer with the relief effort a month earlier. Much of my energy and awareness that had been broadly-focused on the hurricane victims whom I encountered transitioned to laser-like concentration on my writing. This step seemed logical, as a means of aiding interpretation of my two weeks by raising money for the hurricane victims and extending the benefit of the experience by sharing it with anyone interested.

It was not until I began the process of writing this memoir that I learned how advantageous it would be towards understanding my Red Cross experience. More precisely, it was the process of writing a memoir with the intent to publish it, which stimulated the spiritual interpretation of the experience. With this being my first venture into professional writing, I found that writing for a group of readers fundamentally altered—and enhanced—the quality of my writing. The very intent to engage my readers at a higher level elevated my entire writing experience from a static process of simply relating the spiritual growth that I had experienced during a specific two-week time period to a dynamic process in which new insights and growth continued to occur. In sharp contrast to a more conventional pattern where the insights from an experience gradually fade with time, my decision to maintain an outward focus actually fortified those revelations and fostered new ones that would not have otherwise occurred. It became a fertile bed for reinforcing the spiritual value of genuinely reaching out to others.

Along the way, it occurred to me that the external, feeling-oriented action of sharing my thoughts and emotions with an imagined audience of readers was replicating my actions in Gulfport for a very tangible audience of hurricane victims. And, most noteworthy, in both cases this action catalyzed spiritual insight and growth. I reasoned that the common element was the fact that I was acting in direct opposition to my personality and pattern of being more internal and thinking-oriented. In previous study, I had learned that one of the eminent psychotherapist Carl Jung's most significant insights was how a person's inferior (meaning less utilized) function is closely connected with the deeper levels of the soul. For example, with my predisposition towards thinking, an action that is more feeling-oriented such as art or dance has more direct access to the deeper levels of my unconscious and soul, and correspondingly has the potential to be a vehicle for messages and insights from deep within myself. One particularly influential book that I had previously read on this topic was *Discovering Your Soul's Purpose*, by Mark Thurston.[1] In that book, Thurston describes how incorporating such actions into a spiritual discipline can be very instructive in determining the ideal of your soul and its intentions for your life.

Although I had not intentionally engaged in the feeling-oriented actions of assisting others in emotional duress as a spiritual discipline, doing so nonetheless had the same effect. With additional reflection, I realized that the spiritual benefit was undoubtedly enhanced by the fact that these specific, feeling-oriented actions connected me—emotionally and spiritually—to others in a way that other feeling-oriented actions like art or dance might not. As a result, I learned what felt like a crucial spiritual insight: in order to grow spiritually, it is essential that I take the risk to open my heart and reach out to others with words and actions that connect emotionally and spiritually.

# 7

## *Divine Involvement*

*Unless you assume a God, the question of life's purpose is meaningless.*

*—Bertrand Russell*

The first month or two of writing—much of it done at the end of work days with the boys asleep—went quickly and smoothly. It was a straightforward procedure of transferring my steno-pad scribbled notes onto the computer screen and building them into coherent pieces. The remaining daunting challenge was to unite those disparate fragments into a consequential and enjoyable story. Actually, I foresaw two stories: the bigger picture narrative of my experience in Gulfport, as well as a more reflective sub-story about how the experience affected me, especially in relation to my search for a greater sense of purpose in life. The binding agent for the fragments now on my computer screen and the eventual two stories was undoubtedly the meaning and significance imbedded within my experience. Although I was certain of the existence of that substance, it still needed to be extracted from what was now a pile of gold ore.

After I completed the easier first phase of recording the fragments of journal entries, I began to struggle with not only what to write, but the very process of writing itself. Trying to find a productive balance between a linear, cognitive approach versus an intuitive, more spiritual approach was paralleling my struggle with the process of discerning a sense of purpose for my life. From the outset, my writing project was not limited to a distinct and isolated portion of each day. It was not as if I was so preoccupied with my writing that my work and relationships suffered, but it was always at least simmering on the back burner of my thoughts, emotions, and subconscious. Given that I was open to intuition, revelation, and whatever the universe brought my way and with my entire being permeated with my writing endeavor, many actions and events transpired that eventually became connected in various ways to my memoir-writing. As a result, the book-writing, the book-writing process, and the rest of my life became so intertwined as to be inseparable.

Here is one example of that entanglement of my book-writing and seemingly trivial events. One day while getting my hair cut, the only available magazine of interest was an issue of *Rolling Stone.* I randomly opened it up to the first page of an article about the rock musician, Neil Young, which I proceeded to read. About halfway through the article, the author/interviewer asks Neil Young about his process for creating music, and he responds, "I don't so much write the music, as the music is revealed to me."[1] He sees himself as the conduit, with some entire songs coming to him in 30 seconds.

Later that same day a friend and I were discussing some aspect of faith, and he lent me a copy of an essay entitled "Faith and Fiction" by Christian author, Frederick Buechner.[2] In the essay, Buechner expresses his view that fiction-writing and faith have the same raw materials: "the things that have happened to you and the things you've dreamed of happening." He continues that, "if you're a writer, you try less to impose a shape, than to see what shape emerges from it." Explaining further, Buechner writes, "And if minor characters show an inclination to become major characters, as they're apt to do, you at least give them a shot at it, because in the world of fiction it may take many pages before you find out who the major characters really are, just as in the real world it may take you many years to find out that the stranger you talked to once for half an hour in the railway station may have done more to point you to where your true homeland lies than your priest or your best friend or even your psychiatrist."

Reading both pieces on the same day initiated a comparison in my mind. Although I am awestruck at the reality and mystical quality of a song being revealed to a musician, I can understand that it occurs. On the other hand, the concept of a fiction writer creating a story by means of revelations about what his characters *want to be*, is nearly incomprehensible to me. Even though absolutely considering writing—especially fiction—to be a creative process, I still thought of writing as being a more cognitive and calculated art form, in comparison to music. "How does my writing and the approach I'm taking stack up against that?" I pondered. My first thought was the clarification that I was writing nonfiction, rather than fiction, so it therefore required a more linear and cognitive approach. On the other hand, I self-rebutted, it was more specifically a memoir with an introspective and spiritually-oriented flair.

At that moment, I realized that two seemingly innocuous actions—picking up a magazine and opening it at random and having an article lent to me without my requesting it—had uncannily coalesced to bring me back to the crucial issue of not only my writing, but also my search for purpose. In both endeavors, I was making a determined effort to be more open to intuition and revelations, and here was a revelation reminding me of that.

Over the course of the six months of my writing, there were as many of these occurrences of meaningful coincidence as I had experienced in all of my previous years. There is a term for such events, and it is synchronicity. The concept of synchronicity was developed largely by psychiatrist Carl Jung, who credited Albert Einstein as his inspiration for the concept. He defined it as "a non-causal connecting principle that links seemingly unrelated and unconnected events."[3] Examples include thinking of someone for the first time in years and then running into them a few hours later, hearing an unusual phrase you'd never heard before three times in the same day, or having a book fall off a shelf at the bookstore and it's exactly what you need. There are people who interpret these synchronistic events in their lives as evidence of a higher level of existence and as a potential means of communication from God. They believe that there is a spiritual force directing such events and that there is an imbedded lesson to be learned or direction to follow. The concept is integral to Eastern philosophy, but it is contrary to the cause and effect underpinning of Western thought. In the West, with its rational-based "five senses and that's it" paradigm, such coincidences are popularly discounted as chance happenings.

So how do we know which it is, just a chance happening or God's way of remaining anonymous? Once again, Frederick Buechner, has written an insightful response. He recognizes that we can never be absolutely certain, "because the evidence both ways is fragmentary, fragile, and ambiguous." "Whether we bet 'yes' or 'no'," he continues, "is equally an act of faith." The important point, however, is that "We all bet, one way or the other, and it's our lives themselves we're betting with, in the sense that the betting is what shapes our lives."[2]

Closely related to synchronistic occurrences are acts of grace. The word *grace* has at least eight meanings, all of them positive and poetic. In this case, I use the term to mean divine protection, gifts, and guidance. "Blessing" would be another term for it. During my time in Gulfport, and throughout the period of reflecting upon and writing about it, grace was bestowed upon me. In my view, I was the recipient of this grace due to my seeking with all my mind, heart, and soul to discern a divine purpose for my life, and to follow that path, just as it would be bestowed upon anyone else seeking their own divine purpose. These occurrences that I interpreted as having sacred origin were typically incidences that served to provide me with exactly what I needed, and when. They would arrive unexpectedly, with a variety of messengers, by means of actions that initially seemed trivial. Here are some examples to give you a better idea of what I mean. Early on in my writing, I initiated an email conversation with a friend, Susan Skog, who is a very accomplished writer and speaker on the topics of spirituality, peace-making, and living with compassion. In seeking her input for my writing, I mentioned my idea of uniting my memoir with a theme of searching for meaning, because I had observed many of the hurricane victims struggling with similar searches, and my going to Mississippi was clearly a part of my own similar quest. In this same email, I happened to mention that this idea had come to me after waking up from a nightmare of being in a hurricane. In Susan's responding email, she pondered what the symbolic meaning of a hurricane is in traditional psyche/psychological explorations. She wondered, as she put it, "if there is a way of using that hurricane analogy to describe the connection between the upheavals that occur in the natural world and our own inner world with 'hurricane-like' events—such as in a spiritual quest or search for meaning."

That idea struck me as a very intriguing topic to explore, so I did a quick *Google* search on "psyche hurricane tornado dream analysis." That search came back with 23,000 matches, and the *first* one listed was www.marthablake.com. I clicked on that listing, and my eyes were immediately drawn to the following statement in the second paragraph: "The earliest myth known to humankind is the account of a natural disaster…. It is the story of a tumultuous clash of warm and cold forces—of Nature and human nature—and of archetypal devastation and suffering. It is the earliest known invitation to search for meaning in the ways we suffer and help each other through the storms of life."[4] With the proverbial chills down my spine, I recognized it as a fantastic epigraph for the first chapter of my manuscript. Better than anything I could have imagined, this quote from Martha Blake—a Portland-based Jungian analyst who studies dream imagery and mythology—expertly tied together the somewhat disparate sub-themes of my manuscript, those being a hurricane, a search for meaning, and the providing of assistance to others in crisis.

I read on in her website. The second statement that I read regarding the symbolism of a hurricane said, "Getting past the turbulence entails finding meaning. Just as the body metabolizes food to create nourishment, the mind processes raw experience into thoughts to make meaning. To weather emotional storms the resilient psyche searches and finds meaning in the storm."[4] The victims of Katrina had a very real hurricane that created their raw experience from which to find meaning. Although certainly not as agonizing, my raw experience consisted of being deeply affected by dozens of these victims' stories and then helping them to recover. That statement spoke directly to me about my personal need to continue to process my experience into meaning through reflection and the writing of a memoir for publication. When I contacted Martha Blake to ask her permission to use these quotations, she informed me that she was also a Red Cross volunteer and that she would gladly agree to my use of the material.

On more than a dozen additional occasions, I received words of encouragement and pieces of advice, or happened upon a relevant and beneficial statement, precisely when I needed it the most. As one last example, there was another string of events that proved helpful. It began with my reading a posting on Curt Rosengren's Occupational Adventure website.[5] In a posting that described the correlation between happiness and making a difference, there was a link to a blurb on a book entitled *Zen and the Art of Living*, by Laurence Boldt. On a whim, I decided to buy it. When I received it, I read the back cover, scanned the table of contents, and then opened to an inner page, at random, just to get a feel for the style and content. On that page, there happened to be a boxed essay entitled "The Art of Everyday Living" that applied the analogy of an artist creating a work of art to one's creating the life that one wants. The first two sentences that I read were these: "If you have twelve crayons in your box, use your creativity and resourcefulness to make the best picture you can with these. Don't spend your time worrying that someone else has forty-eight or sixty-four crayons."[6] The analogy of the artist resonated with me, and the words were exactly the encouragement that I needed because I had been self-critical in comparing myself to other writers.

After many such instances, I reflected upon the implausibly advantageous nature of them, and how they had bolstered—and even led—my efforts. Even in my most skeptical and rationality-dominated moments, I would be hard-pressed to think of these happenings as nothing more than chance, with no level of higher meaning or manifestation of a Higher Power. My perspective, even if I were to disregard the spiritual context of all that I had experienced during this time, was that these were occurrences of synchronicity and God's grace. I chose to interpret them as an affirmation of the approach that I was taking.

I finally concluded that another level of benefit could be derived from these events. The synchronicity and grace, in and of itself, was a story worth telling. The very fact of its existence as a possible means of communication from God was an invaluable lesson. I thought of the many methods through which I have felt God offer guidance to me in my life: as a result of answered prayers and insights gained during meditation, by means of the bliss that sometimes inexplicably wells up from my soul, and even occasionally through other people's words and music. How should I apply this principle? First, I need to spiritually prepare myself and foster the right environment to catalyze the potential for messages of this sort. Second, I need to be spiritually tuned in and sensitive enough to be able to perceive these messages. And third, when I am blessed with such guidance, I need to have the faith and courage to follow it.

# 8

# *Some Resolution*

*God doesn't look at how much we do, but with how much love we do it.*

—*Mother Teresa*

Not until late March of 2006 did I complete the first draft of the manuscript. By that time, the Red Cross had effectively ended its services related to Hurricane Katrina, with the focus now shifted to FEMA and other longer-term relief agencies and groups. That closure enabled me to obtain current and accurate figures for the overall impact of the Red Cross on the Katrina relief effort. The statistics were astounding. Over $2 billion had been raised and expended by the American Red Cross in assisting an estimated 3.7 million hurricane survivors with shelter/ temporary housing, meals, mental health and medical care, comfort and clean-up supplies, financial assistance, and/or assistance in locating an evacuee. Most extraordinary to me were the statistics that 219,500 people had volunteered with the Red Cross and operated 1,100 shelters across 27 states.[1] Those figures served to yet again indicate the incredible magnitude of the hurricane's impact. Additionally, the remarkably high numbers of Red Cross volunteers and the numbers of shelters spread over half of the country reminded me how extremely fortunate I was to have assisted in one of the relatively few shelters on the front line.

From my research into the Red Cross at this time, it was also very encouraging to learn that they were already well into the process of debriefing, and working towards implementing changes based upon lessons learned during the Katrina relief effort.

During the late fall, I also began the process of sending query letters to literary agents and publishers, hoping to interest them in my writing. Offsetting the increasing discouragement of the inevitable string of rejection letters was the pleasure of communication with the people most influential to my experience in Gulfport. From the very beginning of writing my journal, I thought it would be beneficial—from a story-telling perspective—to include an update on the people I had met and the organizational partnerships that I had attempted to facilitate. In addition to that motivation, I was extremely curious to know of the personal stories and outcomes. I was hoping and praying for the best.

I was disappointed but not surprised to learn from Dave, my physician friend in Kansas City, that his commendable effort to relocate veterans from the Mississippi coast to his V.A. domiciliary had floundered. Apparently, the bureaucracy and inertia were too formidable to overcome. Although I know that he was disappointed, I hope that Dave still felt good about his effort. And one never knows what future actions can result from an attempt that initially fails. Perhaps Dave's actions nudged a higher-level administrator's consciousness just enough so that he or she will answer affirmatively to the next opportunity for a novel approach that provides benefit.

It was also somewhat discouraging to learn that my efforts to initiate charitable donations from the First United Methodist Church in Fort Collins to the Methodist church in Gulfport had not reached fruition. Having witnessed the extreme need and urgency first-hand, I had hoped—perhaps naively—that a church would be a viable option for providing financial assistance quickly, without the bureaucracy of a governmental agency or a large non-profit organization. Understandably though, they needed to go through their established decision-making process to assure that any donations were accountable and in alignment with the objectives for their outreach ministry. As it turned out, they decided to donate about $12,000 to the United Methodist Committee on Relief, with a portion of that designated for the general Hurricane Katrina and Rita relief efforts. And who knows, maybe in the long run those funds will go towards a relief-related need that is equally or even more urgent. I had learned that the degree of urgency is not necessarily directly proportional to the number of days after the hurricane hit. It is possible for some relief-related issues to be well under control for a few weeks or even a few months after the hurricane, with more media attention and funding focus, and then suddenly mushroom into a critical need later on after funding runs out and volunteers leave.

The next update that I received, in late October, was nothing short of exhilarating. This news came from conversations with Ray Caraway, the executive director of the Community Foundation of Northern Colorado, and Donna Alexander, the executive director of the United Way of South Mississippi. While I had been in Gulfport, I had learned that Ray needed the names and phone numbers of contact people on the Mississippi coast who could help him to identify local non-profit agencies which would be appropriate recipients of a portion of the $2 million that had been raised in Fort Collins for the hurricane relief. With land lines down and cell phones still not working well on the coast, it would have been difficult for Ray to accomplish that task. I had put Ray and Donna in touch with each other. Now, Ray told me that he and Gordan Thibedeau, the executive director of the United Way of Fort Collins, had completed a second trip earlier in October to the Louisiana and Mississippi coasts to research and distribute funding. Their first stop on the Mississippi coast was in Waveland, a community about 20 miles west of Gulfport, an area that had suffered the strongest winds and highest storm surges. They were able to identify appropriate hurricane relief agencies and a foundation in Waveland through contacts made by Geoff Smith, a Fort Collins' developer/builder who had personally donated many weeks and thousands of dollars to assist in Waveland.

Ray and Gordan had then moved on to Gulfport to meet with Donna Alexander and to tour the area. Donna provided them with suggested local non-profit groups that could most directly, quickly, and effectively resolve social needs left by the hurricane. By the time they left, checks totaling $283,000 had been distributed to a variety of programs in urgent need along the Mississippi coast from Bay St. Louis and Waveland on the west to Gulfport and Biloxi on the east. Among the beneficiary programs were emergency services, a Head Start program for the children of working mothers, a new in-school program offered by a Boys and Girls Club that had lost their building, and the reconstruction of a food bank building. I was favorably impressed that Donna was clearly focused on providing recommendations to Ray and Gordan that were in the best interest of her region and not necessarily her United Way agency. All of the donated funds went directly to the respective non-profit groups, rather than being funneled through her United Way. Furthermore, several of the agencies/programs that she recommended were not currently affiliated with the United Way. It was extremely gratifying to know that I had been able to play a very small but critical part in making all of that happen.

# 9

# *In Touch with Volunteers*

Four weeks after returning, I began missing the camaraderie of the wonderful Red Cross volunteers whom I had met, so I began to send emails to those with whom I felt closest and had the most interest in finding out how they were doing.

When I had last seen Jill, she was frantically leaving the Gulfport Central Elementary School shelter to catch a plane. At that point, there was still the worrisome issue of whether or not she had contracted hepatitis through the accidental stick from a lancet that had just been used by a diabetic client with hepatitis. Jill had suspected that it was non-contagious alcoholic hepatitis that the client had, rather than the very serious, contagious hepatitis C. Still, she needed to have blood tests taken to assure that. When I received an email response from Jill, she shared the extremely good news that she had had several blood tests since returning, and all of them had been negative for hepatitis C. To play it safe, she had also checked for HIV, since the client might not have been forthcoming about that, if she were HIV-positive. Fortunately, that test also came back negative. In one of my emails to Jill, I asked her the open-ended question of how the overall experience of managing the Red Cross shelter in Gulfport had affected her. More specifically, I wondered if it had catalyzed any transformations in her life. She was kind enough to answer, with much reflection and detail. Jill had been deeply moved by the resiliency of the hurricane victims in making the best of such tragic circumstances, as well as by the Red Cross volunteers who worked tirelessly without complaining. It was amazing to her (as it was to me) that a dozen or more volunteers from all over the country, from many different walks of life, could so easily coalesce into such a productive and positive team under such stressful and demanding conditions. They had earned her utmost respect and admiration, and she was truly inspired by what she witnessed.

There is an adage that we never know how we will respond to a crisis until we are confronted with it. Although we would like to think we know, imagining ourselves in a major crisis is completely different than facing live bullets. With the surreal and ultra-stressful environment that Jill was thrust into, she learned a lot about herself. She discovered that her endurance was greater than she would have thought, stating, "I called on every ounce of energy and strength that I had, and then somehow reached into myself for more." With a vertical learning curve in front of her, she used her known skills, and rapidly acquired new ones. Not only did she gain a better sense of her strengths, she said that she also learned about some weaknesses. In a more spiritual vein, she came to trust that whenever the situation seemed untenable and help was really needed, the help would appear. On more than a few occasions, when she thought she was at the absolute end of the rope, the needed supplies, equipment, or people would arrive, as if on cue. When Jill returned to her normal life, she continued her Red Cross involvement through her local chapter, and took on additional training and volunteer assignments. She became a member of her chapter's Disaster Action Team, responding to various local disasters, primarily house fires. Then, in January, she had decided to leave her position as the manager of a domestic abuse and sexual assault shelter to accept an offer as the Director of Emergency Services for her local Red Cross chapter. In retrospect, she saw it as a natural progression originating from her experience with the Katrina relief effort. During those two weeks in Gulfport, she had discovered that she has a true passion for and dedication to disaster services and that she wanted to work in that field full-time. I cannot think of a better person for the job.

It was gratifying to reach Carrie, the nurse from San Francisco with whom I had enjoyed time early on in my deployment. With other Red Cross volunteers that I had felt closest to, there had been at least the opportunity for a modicum of closure, in saying goodbye, expressing sentiments, and exchanging contact information. I had not had that chance with Carrie, but at least I had written down her name as part of my daily note-taking and remembered her place of employment. After I was eventually able to acquire Carrie's workplace email address, send her a message, and get a response, I learned that she had recently returned from an adventure of an entirely different sort. Soon after returning from Gulfport, she had headed to Kenya, where she was successful in climbing the 19,340 foot Mount Kilimanjaro. In one of our conversations, she had mentioned that she had been training for that challenge and was excitedly looking forward to it. While listening to her, I remember being impressed with her in three ways: first, that she was working toward such a remarkable goal of a physical and bold nature; second, that she was willing to squeeze in the two weeks of volunteering for hurricane relief, with the financial impact of lost pay and the cost of airfare; last, that she was that balanced in living her life, with health and fitness, adventure, and humanitarian pursuits.

My purpose in contacting Carrie was multiple. I wanted to maintain contact with her as a new acquaintance/friend, to gain her permission to mention her in my narrative, and to verify the accuracy of what I had written about her. Additionally, I wanted to learn more about how the hurricane relief experience had been for her, and I was very interested in having her feedback on my writing (given that she was a very literary and bright person). The latter was somewhat of a risk, but I reasoned that sharing my written thoughts and emotions with pre-selected people whom I trusted was a good training step for becoming comfortable with sharing them with the general public in a published book.

Fresh back from those two rich and stimulating experiences, Carrie was struggling with extracting meaning from it all, trying to determine how she wanted to apply them to her life—just as I was. She had taken the time to read my draft manuscript and was, coincidentally, also finding solace and value in writing about her own time in Gulfport. As it turned out, we noticed that we were writing remarkably similar stories, especially with regard to our observations and opinions about the external experience. We had both learned quickly about the necessity of being observant and self-directed and of using initiative to garner the desired assignment and to have the most positive impact. From Carrie's vantage point, she had also witnessed an extreme lack of coordination and misinformation on the part of the governmental agencies and the Red Cross, with the resultant prevalence of rumor as a component of most communication. Due to the severe environment—the poverty, substance abuse, and mental illness on top of the hurricane's wrath—Carrie, like me, had observed the speed with which meaningful connections were made between people and the sense of camaraderie that developed. Another duplicated observation had to do with the occasional bickering and territorial battles waged within medical teams comprised of strangers. I had surmised that this problem was more prevalent with the medical groups—as compared with all of the other volunteers—because they had to work more directly with each other and within a more confined space, and they were utilizing their professional expertise to a greater degree, creating the potential for ego-oriented conflicts. Carrie had also detected an ironic self-centered component to some of her fellow medical volunteers' motivation to assist with the hurricane relief.

In response to my question about her motivation for volunteering, Carrie wrote back, "Morbid fascination sharpened itself into shame and the compulsion to play some small part in rectifying what I felt was not only a colossal failure of the government, but somehow a collective failure of the whole voting nation. We have a responsibility to each other in a democracy. I believe that this disaster played out the way it did because of abject poverty that we had either decided to accept as a society, or simply turned a blind eye to." Despite all of the problems with the overall relief structure and process and the associated frustrations, Carrie had also found the work deeply satisfying. The experience had caused her to reevaluate her current employment, because she felt that her hospital had done very little to assist with the hurricane relief effort and that it catered too much to a privileged clientele. She wasn't sure that she would want to work in public or international health for an extended period, though. With her past experience of doing so in India, she knew that not everyone wants the help that you have to offer and that it is essential for you to find satisfaction in working very hard to help a very few. Another need was to provide for her own financial security, because she had only herself to rely on. So, whatever path she chose, it would need to strike a reasonable balance among those values and needs.

Also living on the West Coast was Dawn, who had done such an exemplary job in helping George and me to manage the shelters. Throughout the fall and early winter, I had seven or eight email and phone conversations with her, initially to obtain permission to use her name, but growing from there. My opinion of Dawn as a generous and caring person was solidified when she voluntarily proof-read and edited my draft manuscript, obviously spending many hours doing so. On her own initiative, she also spent time locating various resources to assist my efforts at getting my manuscript published and kindly offered supportive words when I expressed discouragement with setbacks. Dawn had provided all of this help for me—a person living 1,300 miles away and only known through our common experience in Gulfport. I now consider Dawn a good friend—yet another example of deriving benefit from a tragedy. I valued the opportunity to get to know her better through our communications. Her motivation for volunteering with the Red Cross began with feeling frustration at the horror she saw in the news, that seemed to be going from bad to worse. It seemed to Dawn that our government and our society as a whole were not doing enough. As I (and probably many other volunteers) had, she found the experience to be extremely gratifying and rewarding in some ways, yet frustrating and disappointing in others. The former resulted from witnessing the kindness and generosity of people, the latter from the lack of coordination within and between agencies and the fact that this problem wasn't being solved fast enough. She also expressed some disappointment with the few younger Red Cross volunteers who had seemed to place a bit too much emphasis on having a good time—especially with their partying on their day off—than they did with maximizing their opportunity to help others.

What meaning did Dawn derive from her experience and what impact was it having on her life? Before she left, Dawn had already been reassessing her employment and her living location. Her experience in Gulfport intensified that reflection, because it caused her to think about what was most important in her life. By meeting the many challenges of her long days and many duties at the shelters, she gained a greater sense of self-worth. One result has been a decision to no longer work in situations where she does not feel supported and nourished. Witnessing people who had lost so much, as well as living without many conveniences herself for two weeks, catalyzed a greater sense of gratefulness for what she had. Furthermore, she now realized that she could get by with less material comfort. Dawn discovered—as did I—that she had found great fulfillment in being able to directly help people in critical need. She intends to continue with volunteer work that provides that opportunity, although not necessarily through the Red Cross.

From the beginning, Dawn's goal for volunteering was to make a difference, a refrain that is so simple yet so profound in its implications. At its most elemental, that desire was likely the primary motivator for virtually every volunteer in the hurricane relief effort. Having a direct and positive impact on people's lives has always seemed to me to be an obvious component of living a meaningful life. Even aside from the scientific studies that confirm the physical, psychological, and spiritual benefits of living a life that connects with others and makes the world a better place, most of us know that correlation intuitively from within our hearts. Despite our society's emphasis on material gain and self-centeredness, there are contrasting, positive indicators that a large number of people want a deeper life. One need look no further than the incredible success of Rick Warren's book, *The Purpose-Driven Life: What on Earth Am I Here For?*, with 20 million copies sold since it was published in 2002 and over 100 weeks on the *New York Times* bestseller list.[1] Author Rick Warren's message is a creed of self-sacrifice and altruism for the sake of God and charity.

A second indicator of people in the United States wanting a greater sense of purpose and meaning in their lives through altruistic actions is the gradually increasing percentage of people volunteering in recent years, in particular since the tragic events of September 11, 2001. One interesting subset of that is the larger number of people who are using their vacation time to volunteer for humanitarian or environmental projects. While in Gulfport, I thought of my experience as being aptly described by the term "humanitarian adventure." With this activity being something that I fully intended to continue, I researched the topic a bit after returning. I discovered that so-called "volunteer vacations" are, indeed, becoming more popular. Two recently-published books that serve as excellent resources for people considering the integration of adventure and humanitarian or environmental work into their time away are *Volunteer Vacations: Short-Term Adventures That Will Benefit You and Others* by Bill McMillon, Doug Cutchins, and Anne Geissinger and *How to Live Your Dream of Volunteering Overseas* by Joseph Collins, Stefano DeZerega, and Zahara Heckscher.[2,3]

The last volunteer I was able to reach was George, living in Florida. He was doing well and enjoying his full life in retirement. I was especially interested in hearing how his last week at the shelter went, after I left. As had been promised by the Red Cross headquarters, the number of clients at the Skate Park shelter did continue to increase, as did the number of new Red Cross volunteers. George had a funny story to tell about the continuing saga of getting showers constructed for the shelter. When I left, the only shower for the 60 or so people was a crude tarp shower outside the building, constructed by a few clients and volunteers frustrated with the military's inaction in building them, despite their promise. George informed me that several days after I left, the Navy Seabees arrived and built four very nice wood shower structures, set behind the shelter building. The only problem was that they lacked plumbing and electrical hookups for the water heaters. When George contacted the Seabees who built the shower structures, they informed him that they were only responsible for the carpentry portion of constructing the showers, and that the plumbing and electrical work was handled by two separate skill trade units of the Seabees. They had no idea when the others would show up to complete the job. Fed up with the long wait and bureaucracy, George and another volunteer took matters in their own hands, purchasing the necessary plumbing and electrical supplies at Wal-Mart and completing the construction of the four showers themselves after dark. The volunteer that assisted George happened to be the chief surgeon of a major hospital in a northern state, who was heading up the medical staff at the shelter. A nurse on the staff thought that a chief surgeon holding a flashlight to assist the construction of a shower was remarkable enough that she took a photograph of the scene.

After having these phone and email correspondences with four of my Red Cross co-workers, I thought about how good it felt to be in touch and how meaningful it was that our relationships meant as much to them as they did to me. I also found it notable that, other than George in retirement, each of them had either changed jobs or were considering doing so. Although far from a statistically valid conclusion, I interpret that fact as anecdotally substantiating the profoundly positive impact of the experience of volunteering for the hurricane relief effort. All of these changes were being made with the intent of becoming more aligned with their core values and interests. Their experiences in Gulfport had somehow provided the perspective to clarify what was most important to them and perhaps provided the strength and resolve to make the necessary changes.

# 10

## *A Lesson in Limitations*

○ ○ ○ ○ ○ ○ ○ ○ ○ ○ ○ ○ ○ ○ ○ ○ ○ ○ ○ ○ ○ ○ ○ ○ ○ ○ ○ ○ ○ ○ ○ ○ ○ ○ ○

*God grant me the serenity to accept the things I cannot change; cour-*
*age to change the things I can; and wisdom to know the difference.*

*—Reinhold Niebuhr*

My reminiscing with the Red Cross staffers activated an even deeper yearning to touch base with the hurricane victims that I had felt closest to. One portion of the desire was the simple fact that I had become attached to them through the mutual sharing of heartfelt emotions during a time of crisis. The other aspect was the unresolved nature of my experience with them and my need to find out how they were doing. In some cases I had not even had the chance to say goodbye, and in all cases their lives were at critical points and open-ended. It was as if I were nearing the end of reading the most captivating, descriptive, and poignant novel imaginable, and the book was suddenly snatched from my hands.

Still, despite the strength of my longing to touch base with them and find out how they were doing, I was tentative in my initial efforts. Perhaps their time in the shelter was merged in their memory with the whole tragic experience of the hurricane, with all of its pain and misery, and they would just as soon forget about it all. Maybe there was some degree of embarrassment about needing the assistance that we provided at the shelter. They might not even remember my name, given the chaotic nature of the shelter and the fact that I was just one of many people who were—at least initially—strangers to them.

My speculating about those questions soon faded as my focus shifted to overcoming the challenges of even reaching these people. Although it had been relatively easy to reach my Red Cross comrades, it was very difficult (to the point of futile, in some cases) to reach the hurricane victims I had met. I felt as if I had achieved a monumental victory in the cases where I was finally successful.

Over the course of several months, I made several dozen phone calls attempting to reach Vinh, the Vietnamese man whom I had escorted to the Gulfport Airport. My first contacts were to his aunt and uncle's home in Atlanta where he had presumably been headed. After four or five calls at various times of day and on different days, I finally reached his aunt. "Yes, he made it here just fine. He stayed with us for only a few days, though, before he decided to stay with another aunt on the other side of the Atlanta area. That was three or four weeks ago and I haven't heard from him since," she said. She gave me the second aunt's phone number, and I proceeded to call that at least a dozen times over the course of several weeks without reaching anyone. There was no answering machine.

I called the original aunt again to confirm the phone number and to see if she had any other suggestions for reaching Vinh. Her only idea was to try a phone number in California for his mother. After several attempts at that number, I reached another relative living at their home who told me that their family had not been in contact with Vinh for several years. He showed little interest in hearing the news that I had of his experience in Gulfport. I considered ending this search, but I couldn't, because I felt a burning compulsion to talk directly with Vinh and to have some resolution to his story. I tried the second aunt's phone number several more times over the course of a week, and I was finally rewarded with the voice of a woman answering the phone. She spoke with a thick Asian accent. I was dumbfounded to hear her say that she had no idea who Vinh was, despite my asking her several times, spelling his name, and explaining the situation.

It was hard for me to do, but I decided to surrender this battle. I reasoned that I had at least determined that he had made it to Atlanta, so I could feel good about having assisted that successful effort. The rest would be up to Vinh, who had appeared to be a very resourceful and self-sufficient person. Also, there might be a lesson for me in my determined, yet futile efforts to reach Vinh. The lesson was that hurricanes are obviously very disruptive and powerful in many ways, far beyond my excessive need for completing a story and my flawed thinking that I could overcome it with a relentless effort. Making that relinquishment somewhat easier to swallow was a fantasy that Vinh would someday read this journal in published form and take the initiative to contact me.

During a several-week portion of that same month or two, I made parallel efforts to contact Otis, whose hand I had last shaken shortly before he was to board a bus to Baltimore to assist his cousin, sadly dying from cancer. As with Vinh, my reasons for wanting to reach him were to confirm my hopes and prayers that he was doing all right, to determine the validity of what I had written about him, and to ask for his permission to use his correct name. He had written down his cousin's name for me, and through the Internet I was able to find her phone number and address. Knowing the general condition of his cousin, I was somewhat hesitant to call, but assumed that if Otis was there, he would answer the phone for her. I dialed the number early one evening, and it was answered after a few rings by an older-sounding woman with a very weak voice. I recognized it as his cousin, with whom I had briefly spoken while I was at the Skate Park shelter. I addressed her by name, and began by saying that I was calling from Colorado. Before I could speak another word to introduce myself and the reason for my call, she responded in a voice like none I have ever heard, filled with annoyance and grief. "I'm a very sick woman! Why are you calling me?" she said, hanging up before I could even begin to answer her question.

It must have been a full minute that I sat with the phone in my hand, feeling an odd combination of being both stunned and shamed, as if I had just committed a horrible sin. I kept telling myself that I really hadn't done anything wrong; in fact my motive was completely benevolent. Still, her voice kept ringing in my head, chastising me to the bone.

Never being one to easily give up, I overcame my hesitations and called again the next day. Although certainly feeling very sensitive to her dire condition, I reasoned that I had caught her at a bad time and that there had been a misunderstanding on her part. Surely, if she knew that I was the person who had donated a bit of money to enable Otis's going to Baltimore by bus to help her, at her urging, she would at least tell me if Otis had made it there all right, or tell me how to reach him. So, I took a deep breath and dialed her number. I silently expressed to myself the hope that Otis would answer, but it was not to be. His cousin answered with the same feeble voice. I cringed, at the same time that I rapidly began to apologize for the previous call and explain who I was. With even more aggravation and anguish in her voice—which I wouldn't have thought possible—she quickly informed me that Otis was staying somewhere else in Baltimore, she told me to *never* to call again, and she hung up.

There was no wiggle room for re-interpretation of that exchange. Her anger at first baffled me. After all, I had extended myself to provide help for her by putting some money towards Otis's bus ticket. I certainly wasn't fishing for a thank you, but even a semi-polite response would have been nice. After ruminating on it for awhile, I began to soften. Far be it for me to criticize someone's behavior when he or she is suffering from a terminal illness. I'd like to think that I could still be hospitable towards others if I were in that situation, but who knows? I also concluded that there could have been several possible mitigating factors for her behavior. For example, maybe she was also suffering from a mental illness. Or, maybe there had been a falling-out with Otis and she was projecting that anger towards me. With a few minutes of self-counseling, I also reasoned that there was certainly no reason to feel guilty over my actions.

Perhaps buoyed by that therapeutic insight (and, at no cost!) or by my tenacity, I decided I wanted to take one more crack at trying to reach Otis. Obviously, the phone option was eliminated, but maybe I could somehow get a letter to him. Lacking the address of his whereabouts in Baltimore, my only option was to address the envelope with Otis's name, in care of his cousin and her address. Perhaps she would at least be willing to hand him a piece of mail, if he stopped by for a visit. Despite not feeling real hopeful about its success, I thought it worth trying and it would have minimal impact to her. In an attempt to increase my chances of her not associating the letter with me, I left off the return address on the envelope (even though it would still have a Colorado postmark on it). My letter to Otis was carefully composed, starting off by apologizing to him and his cousin for my upsetting her with my two phone calls. Explaining my motives for contacting him, I also included the portions of my draft manuscript that mentioned him. My letter was concluded with my phone number and mailing address, and the expressed hope that he would contact me to let me know how he was doing.

Not surprisingly, there was no response to my letter. Perhaps it wasn't passed on to Otis, or perhaps he wasn't interested in contacting me, for whatever reason. At first, I felt hurt and a bit discouraged, but only for a few minutes. I saw two obvious lessons to learn from this little event, the first being that it was unreasonable to expect each of my sub-stories to result in tidy, happily ever after endings, as if this were a work of fiction that I was scripting. I was living in the real world with traumatic events, complex relationships, and many forces at play. My second lesson, as I interpreted it, was that engaging in acts of kindness should need no external reward or desired outcome. The intrinsic reward of knowing that I had been doing the right thing should be enough—period. I told myself that I could use a little more "Just let it be" to counteract my desire for specific outcomes. Furthermore, who was I to determine what the best outcome would be for situations I knew so little about? Perhaps Vinh or Otis had decided to take a path completely different from what I had hoped for and anticipated, and their decisions had resulted in a far better outcome from a perspective that would be impossible for me to imagine.

My efforts to learn of Trent's current status were only slightly more successful. He was the tall, distinguished-appearing fellow who had occasionally dropped by to use our shelter's cell phone to assist his job search. I was hoping to hear good news about his locating meaningful and satisfying work. My starting point for reaching Trent was a copy of his resume, which he had given to me. For contact information, there was an email address and a Gulfport phone number and address, which I presumed to be his mother's, because he had mentioned that he was temporarily staying there. I sent an email but never received a response. After a week or two, I called the phone number and was greeted with a pleasant and inspirational response-message on the answering machine. I suspected that it was his mother's voice, and the message was, "Let us be slow to criticize and quick to praise." It took several more phone calls over a handful of days before I reached her.

She was very kind and informed me that Trent was now living in Florida. She thought she had his phone number written down somewhere and would call me back later with it. A day or two later she left a voice message for me, stating that she was unable to locate his phone number. A month or more later, I called her again, just to see if she had since received a phone number or address for him or knew more about how he was doing. Again, she was very cordial, but still had no contact phone number or address for Trent. She had heard second-hand that he was going to enlist in the U.S. Navy, but she was not at all certain. Her voice sounded a little flustered or disoriented, but she was being kind to me, so I suspected that it had to do with her either being tired or perhaps upset with the topic of Trent. I thanked her for her time, she offered that she still had my phone number if she received any more news, and we politely said our good-byes.

My futility in reaching these three men brought my thoughts back to a topic that I had reflected upon frequently during this entire experience; what direct role does God play in tragic events and to what extent do we have free will in our lives? There is currently an increasingly popular spiritual/religious belief that everything happens for a reason, along with the corollary phrase, it was meant to be. If this belief is to mean that God's hand directs every single event and action—from the miniscule to the global and from the loving to the horrific—I would respectfully disagree. I do view God as the omnipotent architect of a universe that is incomprehensible in its exquisite beauty and intricate relationships, from the molecular level to the infinite cosmos. Additionally, I fully believe that God does occasionally intercede in our lives, through determinism, providence, and fate—whatever term you prefer—and even through miracles.

My disagreement with such a philosophy centers on the frequency and type of occasions in which God plays a direct role. To begin with, it seems to me that our Maker created a more complex world with additional variables at play. I can't imagine that an unfathomably powerful Supreme Being would be satisfied with a creation in which the infinite number of details and events were either divinely predetermined from the outset or required constant manipulation of a divine Joystick. More plausible to me is a world in which on most occasions, the primary operating variables in a human's life are the physical forces of the world that God created (with probability and chance as a component), along with the human will that God so magnificently bestowed upon us.

Furthermore, I cannot accept that a loving, compassionate, and merciful Spirit would cause tragedy to happen for a reason, regardless of it being for punishment, a valuable lesson, or even greater good. Whether that tragedy is a function of the physical/natural world that we live in (from a child contracting a disease to a natural disaster killing thousands), or the function of human evil (from a single act of meanness to the Holocaust), I cannot comprehend that it would be directed by a benevolent God, even if there is some eventual good that partially offsets the pain and suffering. I would give more credit in the former case to the physical reality of the world that we live in, and in the latter, to our free will being horribly exercised. So, I do not agree with the belief that Hurricane Katrina—with all of its associated misery, destruction, and death—happened for a divinely-guided reason. However, I do think, most emphatically, that there are many positive lessons to be learned from it, especially on the macro scale, such as issues of appropriate coastal development, federal insurance programs and other economic issues, wetland destruction as a contributing factor, hurricane preparation and relief efforts, etc.

Additionally, and more germane to my personal experience, I staunchly believe that Hurricane Katrina created boundless opportunities for goodness, spiritual growth, and meaning. I also believe that some of those instances were meant to be. I see it as God not directly *causing* the hurricane, but rather *reacting to* the fact that the hurricane happened, setting in motion untold tens of thousands of inter-connected opportunities for goodwill, love, and spiritual growth. These opportunities would be presented not only to the hurricane victims themselves but also to hundreds of thousands of others, like me, who had not been directly affected. As is typical in this game of life that God created, those multitudes of people would have the choice as to what they perceived as options and what paths they took.

# 11

## *From Tragedy to Feeling Blessed*

○ ○ ○ ○ ○ ○ ○ ○ ○ ○ ○ ○ ○ ○ ○ ○ ○ ○ ○ ○ ○ ○ ○ ○ ○ ○ ○ ○ ○ ○ ○ ○ ○

*Draw near to God, and He will draw near to you.*

*—New American Standard Bible, James 4:8*

It is a far easier task to prove the extensive degree to which Hurricane Katrina created the opportunity for the enrichment of the volunteers' lives. But how about the hurricane survivors? They were clearly the people most adversely impacted. What choices and opportunities were presented to them for better lives? How could losing nearly all that you own—including items of irreplaceable, sentimental value—along with possibly your job and, in the worst cases, the lives of loved ones, be seen in a positive light? As hard as that is to imagine, I did meet people who were already overcoming (even while at the shelters, a mere two to four weeks after the hurricane) that tremendous setback with courage and acts of generosity. I witnessed hurricane victims who were able to rise above their own losses, despair, and grief to provide emotional support, physical labor, or give some of the little money they had to strangers equally impacted. It was heartwarming to observe, and always seemed to have a repercussive effect of kindness, magnifying itself through additional people and incidents.

While I was in Gulfport, Cowboy, Julio, Clare, and Anna were the four people who most impressed me in that regard. And how were their lives now, months later? Were they able to maintain that same positive spirit, and maintain their footing on their respective paths of recovery? During November and December, I was extremely pleased to make contact with Cowboy. In this case, it was easy to reach him, because he had given me his cell phone number, and there had been no changes. Addressing me several times with a "Sir," he began by giving me a brief update on the shelter situation. Apparently, for the several weeks after I left, the Skate Park shelter had continued to have more safety concerns and rules violations.

In mid-October, it had reached a maximum of about 120 clients, when yet another group of Red Cross staff transitioned in with the intent to turn the Skate Park into more of a typical Red Cross shelter with added enforcement of regulations. The clients who remained had greatly appreciated that change, and the troublemakers left. Immediately following that transition, the Red Cross made the decision to close Skate Park and other Gulfport shelters, then consolidate into one shelter in Long Beach, the bordering city to the west. By this time, the vast majority of previous clients of the various shelters had found transitional housing of one sort or another, including FEMA trailer homes. Two weeks later, in mid-November, that one remaining Red Cross shelter in Long Beach was closed.

I was most interested to hear about Cowboy's physical rehabilitation. When I had said goodbye to him at the Skate Park shelter in late September, he was in a wheelchair and had external rods screwed to the bones of his lower legs. Since he had been in the wheelchair for four months, his leg muscles must have been quite atrophied. Between the fall and early winter I had four phone conversations with Cowboy. In early December he had some very good news to report. "I'm now able to walk without my crutches; not very far, but I can do it!" he proudly said. "There's even more good news," Cowboy continued. "I finally got my FEMA trailer and I'll be able to stay in that rent-free for 18 months. I've now bought two used pickup trucks that I'm rebuilding, and I'll probably sell one to make some money. The best thing is that I've started a roofing business. It's something I know well and there'll be a big need for roofing around here for quite awhile. I've got two employees working for me and they're living with me in my trailer. I let them stay with me as part of their compensation for work." With a well-deserved sense of accomplishment in his voice, he told me that he could earn $100 a day.

Over the short time that I had gotten to know Cowboy at the shelter, I came to think of him as a soft-spoken, polite, and inspirationally courageous man. My opinion of Cowboy was further substantiated by what he was telling me. If I were to simplistically describe what I observed of the emotional and spiritual impact of the hurricane to its victims, there would be three categories. The first group are the people who reacted with (and stayed stuck in) emotions of grief, anger, and bitterness. They were typically the people who also felt a strong sense of entitlement for governmental and charitable assistance. The second category consists of people who were able to avoid the anger and bitterness but still expressed heavy sadness and depression. Although I could understand some of the reaction of the first group, and I could empathize with those in the second group, I was most drawn towards and inspired by, the third group. Those were the people who had avoided—or at least worked through—the negative emotions and were moving on to higher ground. Not only were they not letting those substantial losses get them down, but they were also seeing this difficult time as a vital experience that had catalyzed for them a more meaningful life, in one way or another.

Cowboy's perspective on his experience with the storm, in his exact words, was that "the hurricane was a blessing in disguise." He felt the same way about the bad construction accident that landed him in a wheelchair for five months and would undoubtedly leave him with discomfort and physical limitations for the rest of his life. "Falling off the roof was a blessing, a wake-up call to get my life in order," he shared in our conversation. Prior to the accident, and for a while thereafter, he had struggled with alcohol addiction. Cowboy reported to me that he had found all of the support and strength that he needed in a local church group and that he had not had a drink for several months. He fully attributed his strength to his belief in Jesus. As we ended our phone conversation, he said to me, "God is good."

In December, I began an effort to reach Julio. As with all of the other hurricane victims, it would take several steps and there would be no assurance of success. I had written down his cell phone number when I last saw him in front of the Skate Park shelter. At that time, he was despairing over his damaged car, which he was towing behind a rental truck. The incident had—at least temporarily—impeded his relocating to Miami, where his sister lived. That cell phone number was no longer valid, so my next recourse was emailing Donna, one of the Red Cross volunteers at the shelter who had established a friendship with him. Donna promptly returned my email, and gave me Julio's last name, as well as his sister's name. With that information, I was able to track down a mailing address for his sister.

Soon after that, I mailed a letter to Julio, in care of his sister. In my letter I introduced myself (being not certain if he would remember me), told him that I was interested in knowing how he was doing and that I was hopeful he was recovering rapidly. I also asked him if I could have his permission to include his story in my book. Additionally, I included the draft of what I had written about him so that he could determine if it was accurate and acceptable.

On January 1st, in the midst of preparing a holiday meal, I had an unexpected phone call. "Hello, Jim? This is Julio!" He was calling from Orlando. Julio explained his circumstances by saying, "Orlando has better job opportunities than Miami for my house-painting skills and they also have better social services to help me get back on my feet. I'm renting an apartment and getting by on FEMA and unemployment checks." Julio was quick to emphasize, however, that, "I'm doing everything I can to get a job so that I don't have to use the government support much longer. Every day I go to the unemployment office and I have several possibilities I'm looking into."

Julio spoke with tremendous energy and excitement. Over the next 30 minutes he expressed more words of appreciation to me than I typically receive in a month (and I don't consider myself to be appreciation-deprived). Julio went on and on about how thankful he was for me, Donna, and our Red Cross staff, for the fact that I was telling the story of the hurricane and its victims in Gulfport, for my inclusion of his story as part of the book, and for my taking the initiative to contact him. With no hesitation, I would say that if I had not received another single word of appreciation from any other person for my two weeks in Gulfport, that one phone call from Julio would have made it all worthwhile.

Julio told me that my letter touched him "real deep" for several reasons. Apparently, some of the people whom he was meeting in Orlando were not aware of the extent of the losses that he had suffered in the hurricane. They were skeptical of his need for government support. On more than a few occasions, he had pulled from his back pocket my letter, now crumpled from extensive use, to provide some degree of documentation. Also, he felt that by my including his story in my book (and informing him of that in my letter) somehow gave more meaning to his tragic experience and the benefit that could come from it. Furthermore, he was so inspired by my taking the leap to write a book that he felt emboldened to do the same. For several years, he had been thinking that he had an important story to tell about his life. He dreamed of writing about it. Julio was starting to write a little bit each day and was excited about the process.

Hearing how he was inspired by my actions rekindled my motivation to find a publisher. Although not at all unexpected for a first-time writer, I had not yet received any positive interest from a literary agent or publisher, and my flame was flickering. I had naively hoped that the previous string of synchronistic and beneficial signs and opportunities would continue. Lately however, it had felt like I was out of the flow. Not that I was at a point of reading into and over-interpreting all of the events and encounters of my days—90 percent of the time I didn't even think about it—but on this occasion, I did decide to view it as encouragement from above.

During that phone call and a few subsequent ones, I learned that Julio does, most certainly, have a meaningful story to tell, and he has the voice and the heart to communicate it. Because he emigrated from the Dominican Republic with his mother and sister when he was 15 years old, English is a second language for him, self-taught over the past 30 years. As a result, he occasionally makes grammatical errors in his speech, and his vocabulary is somewhat limited. However, in a novel manner, Julio is extremely articulate and effective with his English. Despite having fewer choices in his word repertoire, the ones he does choose are often poetic in their combinations, reinforced by the emotional strength with which he delivers them. I suspect it also has to do with the fact that, not growing up with English as his native language, he has not been indoctrinated with the standard word usages and phrases and is therefore free to use them in more unusual combinations without doing so for effect. For example, one of his phrases that I heard at the school shelter was, "I need to get some fresh air in my soul." During one of my phone conversations with him, Julio told me, "I fell through a nightmare, but God caught me."

As with Cowboy, Julio was finding recovery and strength by means of his Christian faith, and he had derived great benefit from attending church. In fact, the first two times that he called me were early Sunday afternoons, soon after he had returned home from church. When Julio talked about his experience with the hurricane, his recovery from it, and his dreams for the future, he consistently expressed his beliefs and his faith. Julio had lost virtually all that he owned in the hurricane, including his job. As a result, he was delinquent on a number of payments and had a bad credit rating, making him ineligible for loans. The hurricane created great struggles for him, and he admitted that he questioned God. In retrospect, he knew that he had needed time to recover and heal from the hurricane's effects. Four months after Katrina, he felt that he had accomplished a spiritual, if not a financial recovery. He passionately stated that the "Lord pulled me through," and he felt blessed. Then, I heard Julio speak words that were strikingly similar to what I had heard a few weeks previous from Cowboy: "It was meant to be that I was in the hurricane."

I was certainly touched by Julio telling me that he was inspired by my actions, but I was more moved by his courage and his vigorous enthusiasm for life, as well as his decision to make the most of it. Julio strongly felt that God had a purpose for him, although he wasn't quite certain of the details. On both accounts, his views sounded like mine. He felt that part of that purpose might be to tell his story of coming from an impoverished country to the United States with all of its opportunities and freedoms that are taken for granted by most Americans. He ended one of our conversations by excitedly saying that he was "still young and strong, and that he had lots of ideas." I can think of no better indicator that Julio was well on his way to being recovered and healed.

Out of the seven hurricane victims that I made efforts to contact, Clare was the only one whom I thought I might be able to find at her original residence in Gulfport. All of the others had moved from Gulfport, and/or had lost their original residence. Making my contact with Clare easier was the fact that I had brought a Gulfport phone book home with me. With a unique last name and Gulfport being relatively small, it was easy to find what I assumed was her listing, although there was an element of speculation, because I only knew the general area of town that she lived in. Also, the listing used only the initial "C" for the first name. I called the phone number for that listing and heard a recording that it was not available for incoming calls, an announcement that was not surprising with so many land lines still being out.

My next recourse was to send a letter to the listed address, hope that it was correct, and ask for her to phone or write me. Several weeks later, in mid-November, I was at work and was surprised to receive a call from her on my cell phone. It was a poor connection, and I was limited in how long I could talk, but it felt good that she was interested enough to respond to my letter. In response to asking her how she was doing, she said, "I'm still struggling with getting rid of the mold in my apartment. Many of my friends and neighbors are still suffering and despairing in different ways." Sad to hear, Clare's news made the point that recovery and healing from such a devastating event is often measured in years, rather than weeks and months.

When I spoke with Clare for a second time in late January, I was relieved to hear that she was considerably more upbeat and hopeful. Although she still spoke of "taking it day by day," there was relative optimism in her voice, progress to report, and she did so with some humor. Although most of her good news was qualified, at least it wasn't all bad. "There's some rebuilding occurring, but the cleanup of damaged buildings and debris is still not complete. Many more businesses are now open, creating more jobs and a better economy. However, just about the entire economy is construction-related, so it's one-dimensional. A recent change in the law now allows the casinos to rebuild on a narrow strip of land on the coast (they were previously limited to being moored in the water), but most are not sure that they want to risk rebuilding. All four lanes of U.S. 90 are now open, but there's not much reason to drive on it, since all of the previous businesses are gone," Clare related.

As for Clare's own recovery, she was awaiting an impending inspection of her rental apartment to determine if it was condemned because of the mold problem. If condemned, it would be bulldozed and she would have to find other housing. When I asked her how her spirit and faith were holding up, she replied, "God still checks in on me occasionally—from sources I wasn't aware of." Her response reminded me of how much I had enjoyed visiting with her at the school shelter, with our introspective, well-thought-out, and spiritually insightful conversations.

At that time, Clare had shared her struggle with not being able to join a particular monastery, because she was older than the maximum age allowed. When I talked with her now about that problem, she seemed to have come to peace with it. Living outside of the monastery, she had the opportunity to "minister in the streets" and more directly serve the homeless and other people who could benefit from the support. It seemed to me that she would do an outstanding job of serving God in that way, with her strength of character, ability to connect with disadvantaged people, and her caring heart.

Also in our discussions at the school shelter, we had talked briefly about the significance of the hurricane to her in a more spiritual sense. She wasn't completely sure then, although she was definitely reflecting upon it. I asked her again during this conversation, about the spiritual significance of the hurricane to her. At least five seconds of silence followed and she began with, "The hurricane was a very big test." I pursued it further, asking if she perceived a specific purpose or mission for herself related to the hurricane. Clare did have a specific response, but by the hesitation I gathered that it was the first time that she had really thought of it that way. Her answer was that it was extremely important to her that St. Thomas the Apostle Catholic Church, in nearby Long Beach, get rebuilt, and she was committed to help make that happen. Clare and about 1,600 families are members of that faith community. The previous summer they had celebrated the 100th anniversary of their beautiful and historic church, which was started by French and Italian immigrants. Their campus also consisted of a recently built Parish Life Center, a rectory, and a school. Hurricane Katrina had reduced all of that to rubble.

Incredibly, she told me they had already rebuilt the school on a site further inland. The local Knights of Columbus purchased the land, along with a hurricane-damaged skating rink. With local and national financial donations and the labor of the local U.S. Navy Seabees, the shell of the skating rink was transformed into a school in a mere 19 days. Despite the majority of the parishioners having suffered major losses themselves, they were pulling together with renewed strength and faith in God and others. They have a website that includes an eight-minute video, with Father Louis Lohan telling this inspiring story.[1] They are now seeing "light and hope" and have every intention of rebuilding the church, Parish Life Center, and rectory. On some nights, Clare goes by herself to the original church site—which now is nothing more than portions of concrete walls—to pray and reflect. While this "very big test," as she put it, is demanding more faith and strength from Clare and the others in her faith community, it seems that they are finding those resources, through God and each other.

Contrary to all of my difficulties in contacting other hurricane victims, Anna is only a local phone call away, having arrived in Fort Collins within a few days of my return. After a month of relocating, she was becoming well-rooted into the community through the sustenance and friendships made in several invaluable support groups. Anna had soon secured an apartment (with initial financial assistance from FEMA) that has a wonderful view of the foothills to the west, allowing her to fully appreciate the natural beauty of this area. By late November, she was earning money doing self-employed housecleaning. In January, she was transitioning to a position as a long-haul truck driver, the work that she had previously done for many years. A longer-term goal of hers is to obtain training and certification as a substance abuse counselor (at which I think she would excel). However, she will need to get herself on better financial footing before she can afford to take that on.

My wife and I saw or called Anna on at least a weekly basis for the first five or six weeks. During that time she joined our family for two trips to the nearby mountains. My admiration for her strength and courage grew as she shared more about her background. In one conversation she told us, "When I was in my 20's I was what they call a 'cutter.' I used knives and other sharp objects to cut my arms and legs. It wasn't so much a suicidal thing, it was just that I wanted to numb my emotional pain." Anna matter-of-factly continued by saying, "A counselor once suggested that when I felt the urge to cut myself, I should heat up a piece of liver in a microwave and rub it on my forearms. I did that several times and it helped. The warmth and the stickiness of the blood from the liver simulated the sensation of my own blood on my skin, and that kept me from cutting myself." Anna is a remarkable testament to the degree to which people can overcome tragic backgrounds through spiritual transformations. Our first trip with her to the mountains was an afternoon drive up to Rocky Mountain National Park, an hour's drive west from Fort Collins. In late September, a popular activity in this area is to go up to the Park to view the incredible gold, orange and yellow colors of the turning aspen leaves, along with watching and hearing the bull elk bugle, a part of their mating ritual. Coloradans who participate in this activity obviously enjoy it, but for locals, though, there is an element of taking it for granted. With this trip being Anna's first experience with it, however, she seemed completely mesmerized and profoundly in awe of the beauty and spectacle of nature's show. I have an indelible image of Anna standing in a grove of aspen with shimmering leaves as the low angle of sunlight illuminated them. Before walking over to the grove, she had said that she simply wanted to be in the presence of the trees and to feel the silky bark. For the briefest of instances, I felt that I was seeing a face of God, observing the miracle and beauty of nature, in conjunction with the miracle of a person transforming her life.

Since then, our contacts have lessened as she has become more settled into the community with other relationships that she has established. It is fortunate that she is such an outgoing, friendly, and self-sufficient person, thus making her transition that much easier.

I have no idea whether or not Anna will become rooted enough in Fort Collins to stay or if there will be a stronger pull to move back to Gulfport or to some other location, for that matter. At times, she has told me that she thoroughly enjoys it in Fort Collins and would not move back. At other times, she speaks of missing her Gulfport friends, and the difficulty—even guilt—of leaving them behind with their continued misery. Two of her Gulfport friends have died since she left, possibly due to complications from hurricane-related illnesses. Regardless of whether or not Anna ends up staying in Fort Collins, both of us have no doubt that our encounter was meant to be, based upon the improbable odds of our meeting and how it substantially altered both of our spiritual and life paths with a feeling of a divine presence pervading it all.

Throughout my life, I have had several experiences—such as a 3,000 mile bicycle tour and a two-month long solo adventure in Europe and India—in which I met strangers to whom I soon felt emotionally close as a result of sharing an enjoyable and/or poignant experience. However, for all of those acquaintances made, in only a handful of instances did I or the other person make the effort to re-connect with a letter or phone call.

In complete contrast to those experiences, I had now been back in contact with seven of my Red Cross co-workers and four hurricane victims. I had made unsuccessful attempts at reaching another four hurricane victims in whom I had strong interest. Although a part of my motivation in making the contacts was for the benefit of this book, the overwhelming motivator was a desire to know how these people were doing. Also in contrast to my previous experiences, the emotions that I felt for these people—while conversing with them on the phone, or thinking of them while typing an email—were just as strong and immediate (if not more so) as they were during the time in Gulfport. The intensity of the experience had been so deep and so profound that the variable of time did nothing to diminish it. From the words that these people shared with me and the emotions we expressed, I have no doubt that they felt the same way about the relationships that they had formed during their experience in the hurricane's aftermath.

# 12

## *Making Sense of it All*

○ ○ ○ ○ ○ ○ ○ ○ ○ ○ ○ ○ ○ ○ ○ ○ ○ ○ ○ ○ ○ ○ ○ ○ ○ ○ ○ ○ ○ ○ ○

*Everyone has a purpose in life; a unique gift or special talent to give to others. And when we blend this unique talent with service to others, we experience the ecstasy and exultation of our own spirit, which is the ultimate goal of all goals.*

*—Deepak Chopra,*
**The Seven Spiritual Laws of Success** [1]

Cowboy, Julio, Clare, and Anna have each reached a point of deriving some sacred meaning—even blessing—out of their experience with the hurricane. Although there was no denying the tremendous destruction and suffering, the hurricane was seen as a wakeup call that realigned them in their belief and faith in a Higher Power. Through that faith—along with their courage and the support, love, and prayers of others—they had found personal and spiritual meaning in not only surviving the storm, but also in gaining a new perspective that was profoundly changing their lives for the better. All four directly attributed their recovery and healing to that source of strength and meaning and readily acknowledged that they would be suffering greatly without it.

There are distinctions between their beliefs, however, that were apparent in the ways they described their faith. Cowboy, Julio, and Clare spoke of being religious, Christians, and attending church services, whereas Anna used the word spiritual, participated in faith-centered meetings, and does not attend church. My interest in this distinction was not because of any agreement or disagreement with their religious/spiritual beliefs whatsoever. I was simply pleased that each of them was grounded in a faith-based belief system of some sort, from which they derived strength and meaning. What piqued my interest in their differences was because of a recent book I had skimmed that was about a national trend. The book is entitled, *Spiritual but not Religious: Understanding Unchurched America*, by Robert Fuller.[2] As the author states, before the 20th century, the two terms of spiritual and religious were used more or less interchangeably. A number of modern cultural and intellectual forces, however, have catalyzed a distinction in the connotation of these words. The increasing prestige of the sciences, the insights of modern biblical scholarship, and the increased awareness of cultural relativism all have made it more difficult for many educated Americans to sustain unqualified loyalty to religious institutions. Many have begun to find more personal meaning with the *private* realm of their own beliefs and experience, rather than with the *public* realm of institutions, rituals, and doctrine. The word *spiritual* gradually came to be associated with the former, and *religious* with the latter.

How prevalent is this trend towards people referring to themselves as "spiritual, but not religious"? Very prevalent, according to the American Religious Identification Survey, which is considered one of the best measures of Americans' religiosity.[3] The number of Americans who claim no religious affiliation, labeled "Nones" by scholars, has doubled in the past decade to an estimated 29 million (14 percent of the population). Most notably though, "None" does not translate to "no belief." Fully 93 percent of those people believe in God. They pursue their spiritual development outside the realm of traditional, organized religion and tend to borrow eclectically from diverse sources, overlooking differences and synthesizing commonalities into a personal belief system. With their emphasis on private experience rather than public ritual, they frequently seek a direct connection with the divine through meditation and prayer.

If I were to respond to such a survey, I would be cast into that group of Nones, with an unwavering belief in a Higher Power and an ever-present, deep connection to that Power through my soul. My personal conviction is that no one religion has exclusive rights to God, and a religion—or more accurately a religious interpretation—that claims exclusivity through its doctrine and/or proselytizing is not for me. Although I find it self-centered and discounting of the beliefs of hundreds of millions of people of differing faiths for a person to proselytize, I can still be open and accepting of their beliefs, whatever they are, for their own lives. Anything less would be hypocritical. From my perspective, whatever their religious or spiritual beliefs—or the lack of them—the critical test is the quality of their lives in relation to others while on this earth. What is the impact of one's words and deeds? How much love, compassion, joy, and healing does one foster in the world? What is the legacy that one leaves behind?

I have no crystal ball to determine the ultimate impact of my two weeks worth of hurricane relief work. That's for God and others to judge. I'd surely like to think that I made a notable difference in some people's lives and that I will continue to do so, through some cosmic ripple effect. With fond memories of hurricane victims expressing their gratitude and appreciation to me, I do feel that my experience was beneficial. I found myself placed in positions with extraordinary opportunities to make a difference, and I believe that I made the most of it, given my abilities and limitations. Also, I know with absolute assurance that my decision to volunteer and all of the actions that I took while in Gulfport felt undeniably right in my heart.

Although it might make a better story if I could honestly report glowingly upbeat, fairy tale updates and recoveries—and projections for recoveries—for all of the hurricane victims that I attempted to assist, that is not how real life with hurricanes goes, even allowing for instances of divine intervention. That is even more valid with these folks, who suffer from numerous additional challenges with employment, addictions, emotional or physical health, and/or family relationships.

Even though there is no Hollywood ending, this story is still about the goodness, spiritual growth, and meaning that can grow out of tragedy. The statistics associated with the good will and positive benefit manifested from this tragedy were no less impressive than the statistics of its destructive power. I witnessed a representative portion of the results of the generous giving of several billion dollars and many thousands of tons of donated supplies from millions of people throughout the United States and the world. As if it was divinely hard-wired, analogous to the human body healing a skin wound, hundreds of thousands of volunteers were doing their best to restore the well-being of their fellow humans. What seemed most remarkable, even mystical, about these uplifting acts, conversions, and relationships was their dynamic nature and inter-connectedness. On numerous occasions, it was quite evident that one person's courage, kind words, or compassionate act initiated a ripple effect of positive benefit, magnifying itself through additional people and incidents.

For the previous 30 years of my adult life, my *modus operandi* for discerning and fulfilling my life's purpose had been cognition and diligence, basically brain and brawn. As a direct result of my hurricane relief experience, I now am determining meaning and purpose for my life more through my heart and soul. By paying attention to my emotions and my intuition, along with fostering and being open to synchronicity and grace, I feel that I have accessed the language of the Spirit. From the first mutterings six months ago of an inner voice compelling me to assist with the hurricane relief, to this day as I complete my memoir, I have felt supported and directed at a divine level. The past six months have not so much renewed my faith in God—that was not wavering to begin with—but rather it has renewed my faith in my ability to access and communicate with God.

When I contemplate the sheer improbability and the transcendent nature of the string of events that occurred, how could I *not* feel closer to God? (1) Seemingly out of nowhere, I had felt compelled to volunteer with the relief effort in a way that I had never even remotely felt before. (2) Despite no previous experience, I ended up as an assistant manager at one of only a few dozen shelters out of 1,100 shelters nationwide in the area hardest hit. (3) I had felt led to assist specific hurricane victims with actions that dramatically impacted their lives, with a reciprocal feeling on my part that I was equally blessed by them, and all of us having the sense that our crossing paths was meant to be. (4) I had been in just the right place at the right time to play a small but critical role in getting $283,000 in donations distributed to Mississippi coast non-profit agencies helping with the relief effort. (5) Returning home, I felt a relentless drive to write a memoir and get it published, in spite of no previous experience at doing so. I have been guided and supported in the process of writing by dozens of meaningful occurrences that have defied probability, ultimately resulting in this published book, thereby enabling the readers who so choose to create even more waves of good will, compassion, hope, and spiritual growth.

# *Notes*

## Chapter 1—Catastrophe and a Calling

1. Richard Nelson Bolles, *A Practical Manual for Job-Hunters & Careeer-Changers: What Color is Your Parachute?* (Berkeley, California: Ten Speed Press, 1978).

2. Mark Sanborn, *The Fred Factor: How passion in your work and life can turn the ordinary into the extraordinary* (Doubleday, 2004).

## Chapter 3—Jumping in with Both Feet

1. February 1, 2006, <http://www.charitynavigator.org/index.cfm/bay/search.summary/orgid/3277.htm>

## Chapter 4—Shelter Transition

1. January 15, 2006, <http://www.ncmissions.org/ministries/response/Hurricane Katrina.asp>

## Chapter 6—Back Home

1. Mark Thurston, *Discovering Your Soul's Purpose* (Virginia Beach, Virginia: A.R.E. Press, 1984).

## Chapter 7—Divine Involvement

1. Alec Wilkinson, "The Open Man," *Rolling Stone*, January 26, 2006: 30-66.

2. Frederick Buechner, "Faith and Fiction," in *Going on Faith: Writing as a Spiritual Quest*, ed. William Zinsser, (New York, New York: Marlowe & Company, 1999), 45–64.

3. January 20, 2006, <http://forums.lycaeum.org/cgi-bin/ultimatebb.cgi?ubb=get_topic&f=9&t=001095>

4. October 14, 2005, <http://www.marthablake.com/T&Habstract.htm>

5.  January 5, 2006, <http://www.marthablake.com/T&Habstract.htm>

6.  Laurence G. Boldt, *Zen and the Art of Making a Living*, (New York, New York: Penguin Group, 1999), 36.

## Chapter 8—Some Resolution

1.  January 25, 2006, <http://www.redcross.org/news/ds/hurricanes/2005/facts.html>

## Chapter 9—In Touch with Volunteers

1.  Rick Warren, *The Purpose-Driven Life: What on Earth Am I Here For?*, (Grand Rapids, Michigan: Zondervan, 2002).

2.  Bill McMillon, Doug Cutchins, and Anne Geissinger, *Volunteer Vacations: Short-Term Adventures That Will Benefit You and Others*, (Chicago, Illinois: Chicago Review Press, 2003).

3.  Joseph Collins, Stefano DeZerega, and Zahara Heckscher, *How to Live Your Dream of Volunteering Overseas*, (New York, New York: Penguin Books, 2002).

## Chapter 11—From Tragedy to Feeling Blessed

1.  February 1, 2006, <http://www.rebuildstthomas.com/pages/1/index.htm>

## Chapter 12—Making Sense of it All

1.  Deepak Chopra, *The Seven Spiritual Laws of Success*, (San Rafael, California: Amber-Allen Publishing and New World Library, 1994), 93.

2.  Robert Fuller, *Spiritual but not Religious: Understanding Unchurched America*, (New York, New York: Oxford University Press, 2001).

3.  Eric Gorski, "Faith freelancers changing spiritual landscape of West", *Denver Post*, September 12, 2004. page A1.

978-0-595-40098-0
0-595-40098-1